W9-ABG-821

Classical Utopian Theories of Education

CLASSICAL UTOPIAN THEORIES of EDUCATION

by ROBERT T. FISHER, Ed.D.

Bookman Associates :: New York

Library of Congress Catalog Card Number: 62-19466

MANUFACTURED IN THE UNITED STATES OF AMERICA BY
UNITED PRINTING SERVICES, INC.
NEW HAVEN, CONN.

For Lillian

CONTENTS

INTRODUCTION

THERE HAVE BEEN, in the history of man, a few who have been stirred by a higher vision. These few have refused to accept the mundane world as the best habitat for man. They have understood, and understood clearly that the dignity of man required the proper setting. These men, the writers of utopias, knew that man fitted into a higher plan and that acceptance of the society in which they lived with its attendant ills would not permit man to develop into the type of person he was in potential.

The utopists were, if anything, completely opposed to cultural determinism. They believed that men were not bound by inexorable laws inherent either in society or nature, but rather were of a higher nature capable of changing and exploiting both society and nature for the betterment of men. Cultural determinism, with its fatalistic concept that man is merely a product of the forces contained in his society, stifles growth and denies man's two aspects that he shares with the divine: rationality and free will. The utopists were of the opinion that each man could contribute to the changing and improving of society. It would be a fallacy, however, to assume that the utopists were liberals asking for social improvement. They were radicals who wanted complete change. Liberals, while dedicated to the proposition that the condition of men can be improved, insist upon operating within and through the existing social institutions. The utopists, in the spirit of radicalism, demanded complete and unalterable change. Only by creating new institutions and agencies, they said, could men live in the manner that their true nature demanded.

The utopist points the way; he is the intellectual leader. He is among the most important persons in society. He is essential because he proposes ideas, institutions, and agencies which never before existed. But while the element of originality is shared by the artist and inventor, the utopist raises originality to a higher realm by coupling it to his striving for excellence.

The utopian writer must utilize all aspects of creativity to present his proposals, for he, as all innovators, desires acceptance of his schemes. However, he is not bound by the demands either within himself, or from society, for the immediate success of his ideas. While this is perhaps a limiting factor upon most men, the utopian personality is such that he is willing to subject his innate desire for recognition to a higher call: the improvement of the human community.

Utopias have been realized, albeit not within the lifetime of the reform writers. The plans have been, to a large extent, actualized. It is impossible to understand contemporary society without understanding the antecedents which in the main stem from utopian writers. There is not a single phase of human life that has not been touched upon by the utopists and subsequently improved. A cursory list would of necessity include the direct influences upon the New Deal by Bellamy's *Looking Backward,* upon the American constitution by Harrington's *Oceana,* upon science, scientific research and societies, and upon university structure and curriculum by Bacon's *New Atlantis,* upon labor by the Leveler's and Diggers. The contribution of the utopian writers in proposing such areas to be studied as eugenics, marital relations, government, religion, and virtually every aspect of human life has been neglected and credit has not been given. There is one area that the utopists have been in general agreement and wherein they have made significant contributions. That is the area of education. It would appear axiomatic that in reading the classical utopias those which were most significant in offering reform proposals possible of ultimate acceptance contained also ideas for a complete school system. The general theme which appears in every classical utopia is the concept that, within the state, education is the single most important agency. Committed to this proposition the utopists necessarily produced educational ideas that were original, relevant and applicable.

While utopian writing contains elements of great vision, visionary writing does not of itself constitute utopian writing.

Many writings share a resemblance with utopian works; however, a classical utopia must be a complete system dedicated to the radical improvement of the human race and be overwhelmingly committed to the efficacy of education as the means to bring about this improvement of human lot.

Necessarily a utopian personality must exist. The writers of the utopias of course possessed this personality. Moreover, there are persons now who possess it. Belief in the perfectibility of mankind, utilizing education as the means, proposing new and startling ideas to improve the condition of man are characteristics of the utopian personality. Society has two obligations to these men. The first is the requirement that one cannot know the history of man and his institutions without understanding the role of utopias, and certainly cannot hope to inaugurate change and develop new institutions without having known what the classical utopists have said. Secondly, it may be said that those societies that hold the utopian writings and utopian personalities in honor are superior societies.

Classical Utopian Theories of Education

chapter one

UTOPIA

IN ORDER TO ESTABLISH a criterion effectively to determine the works which can be called Utopias, a clear understanding of the concept must first be presented.

In general the writers of the utopias were dealing with problems relative to their times. They intended to offer solutions to the difficulties they saw in the socio-political order about them. The writers were men of great vision. However, what establishes their uniqueness is that they chose this particular method, namely, the writing of the utopias, to express their schemes of social justice.

It is necessary that the term first of all be divorced from any unrealistic taints. The utopias are not biting satires written for the amusement of children. They are serious attempts, by serious and well-informed men, to effect a better human life.

The Concept of Utopia

The first characteristic of this concept is optimism. The utopias were written in times of crisis. It would appear that the vast majority of the men during these periods of stress were content to observe the situation and merely to "view it with alarm"! Some men, however, held hope for the future. Their unbounded faith in the future was based upon their faith in the ability of human nature to perfect itself. These men sought perfection in society and in mankind. Optimism is based upon the idea that human nature can be changed. Pessimism considers human nature intrinsically depraved, incapable of profiting from help. It feels that, at best, men can live together in an armed truce. Society, for the pessimists, is a place where men, due to the fallibility of human nature, are forced to live together in a compromised situation. Thus, while Hobbes proposed a new form of state in his *Leviathan,* it is in no sense of the word a utopia. Hobbes felt that society is merely an inescapable refuge for weak men to survive in an otherwise difficult world where life is ". . . short, nasty and brutish."

Optimism, or hope, is fundamentally faith in the future. The utopists could expect help only in this quarter, but the future was not a fantasy used to soften the pain of their existence. It was a positive force, a right and a duty, imposed upon them, and requiring their constructive help in ordering it properly.

Characteristic of this concept is criticism of existing conditions. The utopists had a strong belief in the need for social justice. In examining their contemporary society they were appalled by the social injustice that was rampant. No more succinct analysis of modern capitalism is given than in Bellamy's *Looking Backward.*[1] The whole school of Utopian Socialism is a modern revolt against economic injustice. Its particular form of utopian philosophy culminated in a pattern of revolutions to establish a new social order dedicated to the removal of economic and social injustice.

Criticism of the status quo is not a prerogative of the utopists alone, but is criticism on the highest plane possible in the sense that these authors offered a solution to the elements that they criticized.

The success of the utopias lies in this criticism of the status quo coupled with solutions. Thus, another characteristic of the concept is originality. The writers had set up entirely new nations, and erected governmental, educational, social and economic institutions of a completely novel character. Freshness of outlook, practicality of the suggestions and originality of ideas are characteristic of the writers.

Novelty was not sought for itself. The originality of the utopists was based upon their idea that they were offering goals to society that would actually, and in time, become part of the social scheme. They were writing constructive plans for social improvement, based upon justice, and restricted to a particular form due to the nature of the circumstances in which they found themselves.

The last characteristic of the concept is a requirement that the author be committed to idealism. It is idealism committed to practical results. Epicurus spoke of the highest caliber of disciples being those who carried out Stoicism and aggressively sought to establish it. The utopists also coupled activity with their idealistic endeavors. Two of the men who wrote gave their lives for their beliefs, another was imprisoned, and all were persecuted.

In the minds of some the concept of utopia tends to be synonymous with idealism. However, coupled with the characteristics of optimism, criticism, and belief in the construction of a new social order, utopism becomes a special form of idealism.

Ideas Common to the Utopias

The proclivity of the utopian writers to center their imaginary states around specific elements is of importance to this study, for while each utopia offers much that is unique, there are certain elements that are common to all. On the general philosophical level these common ideas consist of the following:

1. Freedom is fundamental to an ideal state.
2. The state is primarily religious.
3. Education is the basic institution in the state.
4. Justice is the prime function of the state.

Utopists hold that only in the milieu of freedom can each human being reach his potential. Liberty, in the utopian scheme, was not unconditional, it was definitely related to a code of obligations. The sanctions were primarily of a religious nature. The deterrent to immoral behavior lies in the citizen's awareness of his responsibilities to the over-all good of the state. Thus, while the approbation of society acts as a legal sanction, behavior fundamentally rests upon knowledge of the good. The promotion of good citizenship produces the endurance of the state. The educative agencies have the prime function of producing good citizens. Every aspect of the citizen's life is touched and in some way bettered by the educational system. Success in every aspect of life is the aim of education. The schools include courses designed to assist the occupants of utopia in filling their leisure time, in developing their aesthetic qualities, in making a success of their marriages, and in many other ways. Every man, woman, and child is helped to choose the right occupation. Justice for the utopists is defined as each worker performing the type of work for which he is best suited.

These visionary writers are in accord concerning certain general elements in their educational systems. This concurrence is found in the following areas:

1. Systematized and formalized schools.
2. Well-defined curriculum.
3. Equal educational opportunities for women.
4. Character education.
5. Compulsory education.
6. Adult education.
7. Selectivity and guidance.
8. Vocational education.

It is the purpose of the following several chapters to indicate the specific contribution in the above categories by each of the utopian authors. In the main these writers emphasized the vital nature of education.

The History of Utopias

The history of utopias, as does the history of western civilization, begins with the Greeks. The epoch which produced the *Republic* has had consequences felt to this day. The setting of Plato's *Republic* was Greece. The peninsula of Greece extends into the Mediterranean Sea. It was dotted with city-states such as Locris, Euboea, Aetolia, and Phocis. The most important city-states were Athens and Sparta. The Persian War of 490-470 B.C. established Athens as a center of commerce. During this war Sparta's campaigns were on the land, while Athens' campaigns took place on the sea. After the war Athens used her large navy for commerce. Developing into a busy commercial port, Athens thus had access to many new ideas as traders from all over the Mediterranean came to Athens. Such sciences as astronomy and mathematics were developed and encouraged to assist in solving the increase of problems due to the expanding navy. Increasing prosperity brought leisure. Men who enjoyed this leisure began to contemplate problems that were wider in scope than any they had considered before. The traders who came to Athens brought new ideas. Their travels opened up new vistas. Aristotle describes this situation:

> For when their wealth gave them a greater inclination to leisure, and they had loftier notions of excellence, being also elated with their success, both before and after the Persian War with more zeal than discernment they pursued every kind of knowledge.[2]

The fifth century B.C. was the greatest period in Greek history. Its effects are felt to this day. Among important events the most significant were the Golden Age; the Peloponnesian War; and the impetus philosophy and science received from Socrates, Plato and Aristotle. Among other things, the Golden Age produced the cultivation of the intellect and the development of democracy. An important philosophical law was also formulated at this time. This was the law of moderation which allowed the father of the Golden Age, Pericles, to say, "Our love of what is beautiful does not lead to extravagance; our love of the things of the mind does not make us soft."[3] But war came and as it has always done it brought important changes in the Greek scheme. Kitto states, "This war was the turning-point in the history of the Greek."[4] The invasion of Attica by Sparta was a calamity. Coupled with this was another scourge almost as bad in its effects for it took the life of Pericles. This was a plague that swept over Attica.

The most crucial effect of the war was the end of the city-state.[5]

The last period of this century was characterized in Athens by a people weak and disheartened by war. The government fluctuated between an oligarchy dominated by Sparta, and a democracy bent on destroying all elements representing the past association with Sparta. This democracy indicted and tried Socrates. Socrates chose to die, but his indictment was a symptom of the restored democracy.

This avenging democracy was, in effect, mob rule. It set

out to change the nature of government. The choice of the holders of high seats of government and of the courts was done by alphabetical rotation. From this difficult milieu a challenge arose. The challenge centered about the role of the citizen with respect to political virtue and about replacing the polis with a new form of government. This was the situation at the time of Plato. The *Republic* was written to answer the challenge.

The breakdown in the Greek institutions and life stirred Plato to suggest reforms. Plato's answer to this challenge was a utopia. He used Greek forms in order to get his message across, but he used a new approach in his *Republic*. This approach was to use a scientific attitude to determine methods and means of arriving at a social order designed to meet the challenge of the deterioration of the Greek world. Plato's inventiveness and originality was in part due to his approach toward social and political problems, which was to use a scientific attitude.

Plato originated the concept that the institutions of the state, such as government, education, marriage, etc., could be critically examined, and solutions could be offered. Thus the *Republic* stands as a monument in this tradition. This tradition is in effect the utopian tradition.

As the glory of Greece went into gradual decline a new power was arising in the West. By the first century B.C., Rome was the ascending power in the West. For two hundred years the Pax Romana was known in the area bordering the Mediterranean. The concept of one rule for one people as visualized by Cicero was put into effect. Perhaps the seeds of its own destruction were contained in the Roman Empire. In the second century the decline began. No one cause can be given for the decline. In part it was economic. After the mighty campaigns Rome was content to allow its eastern domains to carry on the majority of manufacturing. In part it was social. There was tremendous cleavage between the classes. It was divided into a tremendously wealthy small elite and a large mass of poor people. Cultural and intellectual pursuits were abandoned. At no time during the period of this decline, even up to the sacking of Rome itself, were the people aware of the situation and the possible effects.

However, during this decline one agency grew in vitality and strength. This was Christianity. "Neither contempt nor ostracism, nor outright persecution, stopped the march of Christianity."[6] The fourth century marked the ascendancy of Christianity. Christianity at the beginning of the fourth century was persecuted everywhere, and at the close of the century was the official state religion. This century produced the great Church fathers St. Ambrose, St. Jerome, Leo I, and St. Augustine. The Edict of Milan and the Nicene Creed were also written in this century.

In 410 A.D. this mighty empire was ravished. The destruction was so complete that it required a thousand years for western civilization to be restored. The pagans blamed this destruction on Christianity. They said that the Roman deities were outraged by Christianity being made the official religion.

St. Augustine elected to answer this criticism. He devoted the first eleven books of the *City of God* to this answer. The remaining fourteen books are concerned with an idealistic plan for a way of life that would allow man to enter the City of God.

The *City of God* is a positive utopia whose theme was essentially Christian idealism. St. Augustine saw many evils, but the chief evil he identified was paganism. The *City of God* is among the first of the classical Christian theological tracts. However, it is more than a theological answer to paganism. It is a classic in the utopian tradition dedicated to the proposition that human society can be erected upon a foundation of social justice. When this foundation is realized the City of God will be on earth.

With the fall of Rome the world withdraw to its cave like a hurt animal. Until the fifteenth century the manor was the sole world to its citizens; the major reason being that there was no longer any protection. Without the might of Rome it was impossible to enforce peace. Commerce was ended. Each manor practically became self-sufficient.

Between the twelfth and fifteenth centuries two major events changed this pattern. The Crusades from the twelfth century on opened up inter-regional trade. Among other things this trade introduced the minting of money. Italy profited most from this trade. Italy acted as a middleman for all business transactions. This increase in commerce requiring money and banks produced deep changes in western society. Among the changes was the development of cities. The urban pattern as we know it was born. The cities became industrialized. Workers left agricultural occupations, went to the cities, and became skilled tradesmen.

The second important event that occurred was the Black Death. This plague occurring in the middle of the fourteenth century caused the death of millions of persons. Whole cities were virtually wiped out. This reduction in population plus the increase of industrialization produced a need for manpower. The institution of serfdom vanished. Free labor came into its own. However, this was not a sudden development but rather a gradual process.

The changes from the twelfth century to the fifteenth were principally economic and social. In the fifteenth century the changes encompassed all of men's relations, and at that same time humanism reached its zenith. It became diffused throughout western culture. Man turned from a concern with the afterlife to a preoccupation with this life. For example, art had served religion during the Middle Ages. During the Renaissance art became free of its religious ties, devoting itself to subjects of a warm nature.

Among the crucial changes that took place was the separation of Church and State.

The answer to the problem "what is the end of the state?" had been given by the Church. Some men, such as Marsilio of Padua, Huss and Machiavelli, led a movement which stated in effect that the end of the state is power. The state was divorced from religious values. The state itself developed a system of values independent of religion.

The Church for the previous thousand years had been the prime vital agency in the western world. It had converted the barbarian invaders, and civilized them. The Church had fought war, violence and brutality. The Church had also maintained literacy.

But abuses had crept into the Church. In the sixteenth century there was a tremendous religious revolution. This Protestant Reformation was not only concerned with correction of religious abuses, it was also symptomatic of the changing spirit of the times. However, humanism and nationalism were, also, equally responsible for the Reformation.

The Church reacted with the Counter-Reformation. The Counter-Reformation corrected abuses, gave a new vital spirit to the Church, but also produced a more strict supervision over its members. The ultimate sign of this strictness was the Inquisition. Though the Counter-Reformation corrected many of the faults of the Church, it came too late. By this time Germany and England had accepted Protestantism.

The break with the Church was led in England by Henry VIII. The immediate cause of the split was the Pope's refusal to grant Henry a divorce. In 1535 Henry had himself declared the supreme head of the Church of England. It was in 1535 that Henry had Thomas More beheaded for refusing to give him allegiance as head of the Church of England.

More had been a close friend to Henry. He performed his post of Lord Chancellor dutifully. During the last years of his life he was shocked by the deterioration in the religious and political life of England. The people were apathetic in regard to religion. Henry was usurping power and creating an absolutistic police state. More was stimulated to write a criticism of the abuses he saw about him. He went beyond the level of criticism. In the *Utopia* he wrote a treatise of governmental, religious and educational reform. The *Utopia* is an eloquent plea for religious toleration, democracy in govenment, and education for citizenship.

The conditions that existed in England were reflected on the continent. Two men embroiled there in the chaotic conditions wrote Utopias. One was Campanella, who was imprisoned by the Church in Italy. Rather than being disillusioned by his treatment he wrote one of the most hopeful and visionary utopias, the *City of the Sun.* Andreae in Switzerland felt that fundamentally the answer to the soical problems remained in Christianity. His *Christianopolis* is a treatise upon an ideal society fundamentally Christian and essentially democratic.

Toward the end of the sixteenth century another man, Francis Bacon, wrote a utopia called the *New Atlantis.* In this work Bacon followed the tradition of Plato in utilizing the scientific method to analyze the problems he saw about him, and to determine solutions.

The seventeenth century was characterized by its general secular nature. The gradual secularization of the crucial issues in the political, social, and economic spheres that had begun the previous century reached their climax in the seventeenth century. This movement was led by the impetus to discover the natural laws which controlled these phenomena. Politically, the seventeenth century was characterized by attempts to establish an absolute monarchical rule. Social and economic life was believed to be controlled by natural law. The eighteenth century saw the repudiation of this theory. The natural law of Hobbes and Locke which had motivated socio-political life in the seventeenth century repudiated this theory. This "natural law" was challenged by such men as Bentham, Burke, Jume, Montesquieu and Rousseau in the eighteenth century.

Thus the absolutism of the seventeenth century was replaced by naturalism of the eighteenth century. Rousseau, writing two utopias, the *Social Contract* and *Emile* expounding naturalism, personifies this philosophy.

By the seventeenth century the *Social Contract* was written to answer the problem of political obligation. Rousseau was concerned with maintenance of the citizen's individual political rights and destiny while still remaining a part of commonwealth. Essentially the question was how could man exercise his inherent right of freedom and still associate with the whole of society. In the *Social Contract* Rousseau upholds the idea of the sovereignty of the people and makes governmental institutions subordinate to the will of the people. The *Emile* is an educational utopia which deals with the problem of creating good citizens.

Rousseau is the last of the classical utopists. At the end of the seventeenth century the idea entered the new phase of Utopian Socialism.

This took its direction from the doctrine of Rousseau that man is born good and that society makes him bad. The movement concerned itself mainly with improving the lot of the common man. The nineteenth century saw the tremendous growth of industrialization. Working conditions of the laboring class were indescribable. Children of six worked in British mines. Life was devoid of any refinement. The jungle conditions described by Hobbes were, in effect, the lot of the laboring classes. The Utopian Socialists centered their crusade with improvement of conditions of the lower economic classes. Like the classical utopists, some of theme wrote utopias, but the majority of them put their schemes for social betterment into practice.

The first important Utopian Socialist was the Comte de Saint-Simon. He took part in the American Revolution and witnessed the French Revolution. The loss of the influence of the Church and the breakdown of politico-social agencies enabled the citizens of France to propose a new social order. Saint-Simon proposed reforms based upon his scientific analysis of social development. He proposed a society based upon a single law, namely that all men should love the brotherhood. He felt that the workers would band together and accept and put into practice his reforms.

The organization of the workers, proposed by Saint-Simon, received assistance in its formation by others. Among the most important was Robert Owen. Owen's utopian society followed Plato's closely. He held that education was the main influence upon one's life. In his proposed community he wanted the children taken from their parents at the age of three and raised by educators. In 1826 in New Harmony, Indiana, Owen established a utopian society. New Harmony was designed to remove the three main evils Owen saw in society, namely, private property, religion, and marriage. New Harmony lasted less than three years. Owen left New Harmony almost immediately after he set it up. It had collapsed primarily because it had attracted drifters and crooks.[7]

There were many other utopian communities established in the United States. The greatest period of the establishing of these communes was between 1840-1860. There were about a hundred and fifty such communities at that time.[8] Among them was the Icarian Community founded by Etienne Cabet who wrote the utopia, *Voyage en Icarie.* Another colony was the Oneida Community founded by John Humphrey Noyes. One of the industries connected with the Oneida Community, the Community Plate, is still in existence. As late as 1942 another utopian community was founded in Georgia. It is the Koinonia Farm. The most significant fact about it is that it is interracial.

Utopian Socialism as a significant force begins to play a secondary role with the advent of Scientific Socialism. This was begun by the publication of the *Communist Manifesto* by Marx and Engels in 1848. In this book Marx and Engels attack the Utopian Socialists with the following comment:

> They still dream of experimental realization of their social utopias, of founding isolated phalansteres, of establishing "Home Colonies," or setting up a "little Icaria"—pocket editions of all New Jerusalem—and to realize all these castles in the air, they are compelled to appeal to the feelings and purses of the bourgeoisie.[9]

The nineteenth century was also characterized by the tremendous growth of a philosophy which held that the role of governments was to enact laws to produce social justice. John Stuart Mill best exemplifies this spirit.

The end of the nineteenth century also saw the writing of the last Utopia. This was *Looking Backward* by Edward Bellamy.

The utopias had served an important function for over two thousand years. This function was to keep alive the idea that social justice could be enacted in human society. They served to keep before men the concept of an ideal community, for which men could strive. With the advent of Utopian and Scientific Socialism their role was finished.

chapter two

THE NATURE OF THE CONCEPT IN THE *REPUBLIC*

PLATO WAS THE AUTHOR of the first major utopian work. The *Republic* is perhaps the best known of his works and has had the most influence upon subsequent philosophy.[1]

Plato's utopia was the pioneer attempt to actualize innovations in the social order. In order to effect the new order he had to systematize several ideas. These ideas are: (1) a theory of the state; (2) a theory of knowledge; (3) an educational system; (4) a theory of psychology.

Plato lived between 427 and 347 B.C.[2] Little is known of Plato's early life.[3] His later life was molded and shaped by his master Socrates and by the changes taking place in the Greek social scheme. These changes were partially due to the Peloponnesian War.

The death, or martyrdom of Socrates as Plato considered it, resulted in Plato's change of plans for his occupational future. For several years after his friend's death he traveled as far as Africa, Italy, and possibly even to India. Upon his return he founded the Academy.[4] This point marked the beginning of his fruitful years as a philosopher.

Division of time in the development of philosophical thought is difficult to make. However, it is possible to state that the history of rational thought began when man investigated his world from the standpoint of a critical attitude. Thus we may state that the Greeks stood on the threshold of a new era. Previous to this era men saw the world as a place occupied by irascible forces and unpredictable demons. The pre-Greek world was a world comprised of myths—myths that were constructed upon the worst elements of human nature. Gods, who controlled men, were prone to select favorites among mankind, were often seducers, charlatans, and even murderers.[5] The Greeks scrutinized the world in terms of deducible laws—laws that would enable man to predict, because these laws were universal. Among the first books that attempted to analyze man's social relations to other men was Plato's *Republic.* Plato assumed that the laws which determined human relationships and institutions could be discovered, and more important, could be manipulated.

The central problem of the *Republic* was the nature of justice and the factors that would actualize it in the state. Plato holds that the cement which bound society together was justice. It would appear that justice was the ideal to which individuals and the state should aspire, but justice was not only a goal it was also a method of achieving true harmony in society.[6]

Justice was essentially individualistic for it implied that every man should perform the task he was best able to do; it was also reciprocal in that the state and the person had responsibilities and obligations to each other. The major obligation of the state to the person rests in the necessity of educating the citizens.

Education for Plato was the means by which the philosopher-king could shape human nature in order to produce a harmonious state. Plato held that virtue was knowledge and that knowledge could be taught. It appears logical to state that all efforts to attain the ideal state are possible, utilizing a good educational system; contrariwise, no matter what a state does if it neglects education it can never be improved.

In order to secure the ideal of justice which would in turn result in a harmonious group, each citizen must be "guided" into the social class and social occupation for which he was best suited. Plato stated:

> We have laid down, as a universal principle, that everyone ought to perform the one function in the community for which his nature is best suited. That principle is justice.[7]

The functions of occupations necessary for the maintenance of the state fell into three classes: (1) tradesmen, or workers, (2) auxiliary, or the military, and (3) guardians, or governmental leaders on the policy-making level. This classification was consistent with Plato's idea of justice.

Plato justified this division of functions by means of psychological evidence. The state in actuality was a reflection of the three functions of the personality: (1) deliberative and governing, (2) executive, and (3) productive. The three parts are found in every personality; however, they are found in varying amounts. This variation makes social life possible and consequently must be reflected by various occupations and social classes in society.

> We must admit that the same elements and characters that appear in the state must exist in every one of us; where else could they have come from ?[8]

Plato felt that the character of a society is in reality the manifestation of the character of its people. Thus a society that is war-like is composed of people who are by nature aggressive, hostile and irritable.

> It would be absurd to imagine that among peoples with a reputation for a high-spirited character, (that) the states have not derived their character from their individual members.[9]

The class lines were rigid and well defined and there was no intercourse between them. The services of each group were integrated so that the state could function harmoniously, but the socio-cultural relations of each group, in many aspects, were diametrically opposed. For instance, in the proposed working class, family life was to follow traditional lines, that is, the citizens were to practice monogamy, rear and be responsible for their own children. They would own private property and progress materially according to their own individual efforts. In the elite power group the pattern changes, in that family life was nonexistent. All wives were held in common and children, never to known their parents, were reared by the state. The guardians would practice a form of communism, they would never own property, and even their social life was to be communal as they lived in barracks and took their meals at common tables.

Theory of Knowledge

Plato's Theory of Knowledge, had four facets, each in turn contributing to the whole. The elements are: (1) ultimate truth, (2) opinion, (3) virtue, and (4) the nature of the seeker of knowledge.[10]

The knower, said Plato, apprehended the world in two different ways due to the fact that the mind is constructed to view data the senses receive in terms of appearances, and essence. Data perceived in terms of appearances is called opinion. The essence of an object is absolute and unchanging reality. Data concerned with essence is knowledge. To know "things" is to know only the external characteristics of a particular subject. Two men viewing the same object may see different material. Thus, for example, an object that is beautiful to one may be ugly to another. Knowledge of beauty consists not in knowledge of beautiful things, which is mere opinion, but in knowledge of the essence of beauty itself, of the absolute nature of beauty per se. Knowledge of appearances is sense-knowledge; it is what Kant referred to as a posteriori knowledge. Opinion states the characteristic of something, it affirms sense-data, it is apodictic. On the other hand knowledge "knows" reality; it understands the inner, true meaning of something; it is infallible. By its very nature knowledge can never be wrong for it is apperception of the "real" truth, that is true "idea" or "form." Opinion can be wrong, for while it can know what "is not," it can never really know what "is," as that is knowledge. Opinion is somewhere between what is and what is not. Thus, opinion knows things that have opposite characteristics, and it deals with things in a state of flux.

In a sense opinion may be compared to experiences one receives in a dream. The things one dreams about are not completely real, but on the other hand not wholly nonexistent. Opinion then, in summary, is of things that seem to exist. Knowledge is of things that are unique, absolute, unchanging, above the world of the senses, above the temporal, into the realm of the eternal.

Plato's theory of forms stated that there were general "ideas" that were necessary, in that language must have general concepts in order to convey meaning. For example, all particular subjects belonging to a class possess characteristics common to all. The general class or form, which exists independent of the individuals that come into existence or disappear, do not affect the form. A particular house exists which possesses certain appearances and appurtenances which may be enchanting, insignificant, or downright irritating, depending upon the observer, but all men understand the general classification of "houseness" which exists as an independent idea. That houses are built or torn down does not affect the idea of "house" which is eternal. The forms being absolute automatically exclude opposites, thus beauty excludes ugliness. Beauty, per se, cannot become ugly, but particular beautiful objects may become ugly, or may appear ugly to different people. Particular objects must also have a beginning and an end. Thus such things can never be objects of knowledge. Rather they are objects of opinion; knowledge deals with the eternal forms. Forms constitute the real world; consequently, knowledge of forms was for Plato true wisdom.

The doctrine of forms was important to Plato who held that by knowing the forms we know the Good. He felt that men must know what is objectively Good in order to have a criterion with which to judge actions, the state, etc. While all men should endeavor to know truth, that is, the Good, not all men are capable of an intensive and broad understanding of it.[11] Those men and women who, due to their superior intelligence will benefit by years of study and who will achieve the "vision of the truth" are the ones chosen to join the ranks of the philosophers (the lovers of truth). Knowledge is necessary not only because it gives a standard, but it is important because it was necessary for virtue. Plato contended that right actions stemmed from knowledge, and that lack of knowledge was a lack of virtue.[12] Since knowledge is fundamental to the right-ordering of the state and for the well-being of the people it is needful that all should pursue it. A right-ordered society depends upon the harmonious relations among its citizens, just as a right-ordered personality depends upon the harmonious relations of one's desires.[13]

Good actions are produced by reason. Reason produces harmony by initiating self-control and temperance. Reason internalized justice, making justice no longer just the factor producing a harmonious state, but also the harmonious ordering of the soul.[14]

Knowledge of the Good is the basis for the new society as well as for the new citizenry. Goodness is achieved by logical investigation; it is real in that it is the ultimate form.

What is the Good? It must be first of all established that the Good does not constitute a separate realm of values. It is the universal object of desire.

Plato divided the Good into two related sections: (1) Human Good and (2) Supreme Good. Human Good is often considered to be pleasure, but Plato emphatically denied this point of view and called those persons who believed this confused, for there are also pleasures which are intrinsically bad, or whose effects are bad.[15] Human Good is essentially knowledge. It is a type of insight coupled with wisdom and while it is understanding of the physical laws it is also enlightenment concerning the moral order. Virtue is an essential aspect of the Human Good, but it is virtue in action; unless there is right action there is little or no knowledge, for Plato said:

> You have often been told that the highest object of knowledge is the essential nature of the Good, from which every thing that is good and right derives its value for us. I need not tell you that, without that knowledge, to know everything else, however well, would be of no value to us, just as it is of no use to possess anything without getting the good of it.[16]

The highest Good is the supreme form; it is God. Plato's theological definition of the Good led the Early Church Fathers to call him "almost a Christian,"[17] for he defined the Good as the ultimate in moral goodness and included such forms as justice, courage, etc. He further referred to the Good as the author of human good and as truth.[18] The vision of the Good comes only to a few; after years of training in philosophy there is a sudden illumination, an immediate apprehension of the Good. When one receives the vision of the Good one suddenly sees the pattern for the world, for Plato held that God's plan becomes clear. He said:

> The objects of knowledge derive from the Good not only their power of being known, but their very being and reality; and Goodness is not the same thing as being, but even beyond being, surpassing it in dignity and power.[19]

The techniques that must be utilized in the training preparatory to the vision of the Good were, said Plato, the special province of education.

Plato's System of Education

Education was the most important agency in the state, said Plato, and thus it was axiomatic that it must not be left in the hands of individuals. Private systems of education cannot be relied upon to serve the whole interests. They will be swayed by the dominant interests of those who support the schools. The suggestions of state-supported schools, compulsory education, and state-controlled schools were among the major contributions made by Plato. By insisting upon universal education for the children it was possible to screen effectively the superior students and train them for posts of leadership and responsibility. Further, it was possible to assist all the pupils in job selection.

Education began early in life according to the *Republic.* The state assumed responsibility for the training of the children at the age of three. The children were taken from the home and spent their time in gymnastics and music. The importance of gymnastics was to aid in the development of a healthy body, for Plato held to the dictum "a healthy mind in a healthy body." State-supported schools were also charged with insuring the health of the nation, but it was not Plato's intention to develop a race of prize fighters and athletes.

After the age of ten the student entered into a more intensive and more developed program of studies.

All the students at the age of twenty underwent tests and examinations for the purpose of determining which students would benefit from further education and which students should be guided into vocational pursuits. Again at thirty-five those students who were still in attendance at the centers of advanced education were tested and superior students were then trained for governmental leadership.

Systematized and Formalized Schools

In the *Republic* there is the suggestion for the world's public school system.

Plato's proposed school system was under the jurisdiction of one of the most important officials in the sate, the minister of education. This office was filled by men of the highest caliber for the future of the state depended upon them. "Such a presiding genius will be always required in our state if the government is to last."[20] The director of education had control over all the aspects of the schools. Plato stated, "Students are not likely to make discoveries without a director."[21] The director was not absolute in his role or his decisions; the community assisted him. The *Republic* revealed:

> Men . . . would be too proud to accept the director's guidance. They would be amenable only if the whole community were to conceive a respect for such work and give the director its support. The problems might then be solved by continuous and energetic investigation.[22]

The aim of the schools and of the minister of education was to induce the spirit of justice and of goodness into the minds and hearts of the students. The schools could produce good citizens by giving them knowledge of the moral and physical order and of the supreme Good, and assisting them to develop the habit of self-control.

The administrators of the schools could not introduce change into the schools. It appears that Plato was distrustful of change, and that once the ideal state was realized Plato would have it continue along rigid lines. Change was expressly forbidden by Plato. He said:

> Those who keep watch over our common wealth must take the greatest care not to overlook the least infraction of the rule against any innovation upon the established system of education.[23]

The aim of the schools was to raise each person to the highest intellectual level that each was capable of attaining. Education promoted a love of cultural pursuits, but further it created men who were led my reason. Without reason life was not better than that led in the jungle by beasts. More important, since Plato held that virtue was knowledge, the schools were charged with developing goodness among all.

Plato recognized the fact that women were not to be barred from social standing.[24] That they were constitutionally handicapped was recognized and dealt with in the following statement: "Men and women alike possess the qualities which make a guardian; they differ only in their comparative strength and weakness."[25]

All citizens of the state attended school for part of their lives, while a few attended it for most of their lives.

All children attended school for two basic reasons: (1) only through the cultivation of the intellect could superior citizens be produced, and (2) every person could benefit to some degree from education, therefore it was their right to it. Plato said: "Our own account signifies that the soul of every man does possess the power of learning the truth and the organ to see it with."[26]

Curriculum in the Republic

The curriculum proposed in the *Republic* was closely related to the various stages of education, e.g., elementary, secondary, and higher education.

In the elementary school the techniques used to convey the course material were based upon the Platonic idea that forced knowledge was no knowledge at all; rather interest and free inquiry on the part of the students replaced the more common, stern methods. Plato said:

> All branches of the preliminary education which is to pave the way for Dialectic should be introduced in childhood; but not in the guise of forced instruction, because for free man there should be no element of slavery in learning. Enforced exercise does no harm to the body, but enforced learning will not stay in the mind. So avoid compulsion, and let your children's lessons take the form of play. This will also help you to see what they are naturally fitted for.[27]

The courses taught during the elementary stage included: (1) gymnastics, including all forms of physical exercise and some training in military pursuits such as marching, use of arms, etc.; (2) grammar, which for Plato included reading and writing, learning and reciting epic and lyric poetry; and (3) the humanities, under which were grouped music, literature, mathematics, cultural pursuits and some science.

In this first period of education the main problem was to control the basic physical drives. Plato held that during this period of the student's life the physical will tended to dominate; thus, reconciling both aspects of the child's personality would be a real challenge to the teacher. The problem was solved by relating both areas in "due proportion" in the soul. This is the often mentioned "theory of harmony," or "all things in moderation."

The education of the child began before the full use of his body developed. Children were told stories before they could indulge in physical exercise. In the main these stories were to convey ethical ideas. The education of childhood should lay a foundation of character which would not have to be cut away as years go on, but would invite and sustain the superstructure of manhood.

The first course in the elementary school was literature, and in a sense was also the most important course,[28] for it gave a foundation in the pursuit of goodness and truth. There were two types of literature, true literature and false literature. The works of Homer and Hesiod were in every sense of the word the bible of the Greeks for they contained the source of all information about the Hellenic gods. These were the very books that Plato attacked the most uncompromisingly. He said:

> Most of the stories now in use must be discarded, including the stories in Hesiod and Homer, and the poets in general, who have at all times composed fictitious tales and told them to mankind. The worst faults found in them is the misrepresentation of the nature of the gods and heroes. The stories are ugly, immoral and false.[29]

Since children could not distinguish the allegorical sense from the literal, the works of literature incorporated in the courses had to be closely watched to see that they conformed to truth. "Falsehood in the stories" said Plato, "must be above everything."[30] The stories in the main consisted of the deeds of heroes, and of heroic actions from which the children could draw moral precepts, and from which it was hoped they would learn right behavior. The stories tried to promote the positive virtues, indicating that goodness always comes as a reward for right actions and justice.

The content of literature was important and equally as important for Plato was the form of the stories. The students presented all the stories in dramatic recitations, and they attempted to imitate realistically the pronunciations and actions of the characters. This imitation to a certain extent would cause the student to identify with the character, and because the imagination of children was fertile, the identification could leave an indelible mark upon the personality and character of the students. He said:

> The students should from childhood upward, impersonate only the appropriate types of character, men who are brave, religious, self-controlled, generous.[31]

Music was an important part of elementary education in the *Republic*, for by means of special techniques utilized in its instruction Plato hoped to inculcate a sense of rhythm and harmony which he claimed had a special socializing influence. Plato stated:

> Musical expression and rhythm, and grace of form and movement, all depend on goodness of nature, that is a nature in which goodness of character has been well and truly established. And the absence of grace, rhythm, harmony is nearly allied to baseness of thought and expression and baseness of character; whereas their presence goes with that moral excellence and self-mastery of which they are the embodiment.[32]

The elementary stage ended at about ten years of age, and secondary education began, and continued to the age of eighteen. The curriculum of the secondary school was exactly the same as that of the elementary school, e.g., the divisions of physical science, grammar, and the humanities. However, these courses were taught on a higher level. At eighteen the students, both boys and girls, received military training, and also at this time they were tested to determine their abilities in regards to further education, or occupation. The program of studies followed a pattern related to age:

	Stage	*Age*	*Program*
I.	Elementary school	3 years to 10	Literature, music, gymnastics.
II.	Secondary school	10 years to 17-18	Same as above with addition of mathematics.
III.	Military and physical training	17 years to 20	No studies during this period.
IV.	College or vocational education. Most students were apprenticed, a few went on for advanced education.	20 years to 30	
V.	Dialectic	30 years to 35-40	Principles of morality.
VI.	Governmental Service	35 years to 50	in governmental Practical experience positions.
VII.	Philosopher	50 years	Individual study in philosophy in order to gain the "vision of the Good."

Higher education was concerned principally with mathematics. The first course was arithmetic. The fundamentals of arithmetic were taught in elementary school, using such means as counting apples; in secondary school it was related to military problems, but on the college level the theoretical aspects were emphasized. Plato felt that the theory of numbers would be used to assist the student in the science of reality.

> Since the properties of number appear to have the power of leading us towards reality, these must be among the studies. The soldier must learn them in order to marshal his troops; the philosopher, because he must rise above the world of change and grasp true being, or he will never become proficient in the calculations of reason.[33]

Plato held that ability in arithmetic was related to intelligence, but that those persons who were not endowed with a great deal of intellect could also profit from studies in mathematics.

> "People with a talent for calculation," said Plato, "are naturally quick at learning almost any other subject, and training in it makes a slow mind quicker, even if it does no other good."[34]

Geometry, both plain and solid, was the next subject studied in the college. Plato called it, ". . . the knowledge of the eternally existent."[35] Plato evidently held that mathematical objects were absolute and unchanging. Geometry studied these eternal objects in order to attain truth, for, ". . . it will draw the soul towards truth and direct upwards the philosophic intelligence which is now wrongly turned earthwards."[36]

Astronomy was taught as a part of pure mathematics, and Plato hoped that the study would teach the students to think abstractly, and he felt that that was important for military purposes and for agriculture and navigators.

The last subject in the college course was harmonics and was taught, as was astronomy, as a part of mathematics. Its value lay in its use as a practical example in measurement, and it was useful ". . . as a means to the knowledge of beauty and goodness."[37]

After the ten year period of higher studies in mathematics

the students, who were thirty years of age, underwent a series of tests to determine who would go on to the next level of advanced work—the school of Dialectic.[38]

Plato described this period in this manner:

> Here, the summit of the intelligible world is reached in philosophic discussion by one who aspires, through the discourse of reason unaided by any of the senses, to make his way in every case to the essential reality and perseveres until he has grasped by pure intelligence the very nature of Goodness itself. This journey is what we call Dialectic.[39]

At this time the student came to grips with reality when he could freely discuss philosophical ideas. Previous to this time he was not allowed freedom of inquiry, he was not allowed to question such ideas as honor, justice, etc., nor was he allowed to debate the moral and political law.

Dialectic was the highest form of thinking. It was a result of the years of training in the aforementioned subjects of gymnastics, humanities, sciences, mathematics. Dialectic was the end of formal training. Plato stated:

> We may conclude that our account of the subjects of study is now complete. Dialectic will stand as the coping-stone of the whole structure; there is no other study that deserves to be put above it.[40]

After the completion of the school of dialectic, and after satisfying the requirement of fifteen years of practical government experience, the philosopher returned to the academic life and spent his life in individual study culminating in the vision of the Good.

Character Education

In *Republic* there were many references made to developing and living a virtuous life. The Platonic theory of knowledge included as fundamental the idea that virtue was knowledge, and that lack of knowledge resulted in wrong actions. The specific virtues that Plato wished to inculcate in his students were not extensive. The list included truthfulness, of which Plato said, ". . . . a high value must be set upon truthfulness.

If anyone is caught not telling the truth the rulers will punish him for introducing a practice that is fatal and subversive in the state."[41] Self control, which was essentially ". . . obeying the governors, and governing the appetite for the pleasures of eating, drinking, and sex,"[42] is included in the list along with courage, justice, and goodness. The last virtue on the list, and in some ways the most important, was temperance, described as a form of orderliness, "A control of certain pleasures and appetites."[43] It was a kind of harmony in the soul since the passions were in balance with reason and the demands of society; it was thus a form of interaction between the person and the society. In one discussion of temperance Plato implied that it incorporated all the virtues and due to the fact that he related it to harmony, tended to make it the supreme virtue.[44]

Plato was particularly concerned with the setting in which education took place and in his own school the setting was a grove of trees, the Akademeia. According to the *Republic* the schools were to have the same flexible and informal atmosphere and the teachers were to be persons who were kind, tolerant, capable of creating enthusiasm and, very importantly, they were persons who by their own high standards were capable by their actions of making the children desire to imitate them. Plato described the environment in the following passage:

> We must supervise craftsmen of every kind and forbid them to leave the stamp of baseness, licence, meanness, unseemliness, on painting and sculpture, or building, or any other work of their hands. We would not have our students grow up among representations of moral deformity, as in some foul pasture where, day after day, feeding on every poisonous weed they would, little by little, gather insensibly a mass of corruption in their very souls. Our young people must dwell in a wholesome climate where influences from noble workers constantly fall upon eye and ear from childhood upward, and imperceptibly draws them into sympathy and harmony with the beauty of reason.[45]

Imitation was another technique to assist the student to develop character. From the time they began their pre-school training and continued through the secondary school, the students were to be exposed to teachers of highest caliber. They also read stories of heroes and saw plays wherein the characters were also persons of great moral standing. Plato said:

> They are not to do anything mean or dishonourable, no more should they be practiced in representing such behavior, for fear of becoming infected with the reality. You must have noticed how reproduction of another person's gestures or tones of voice or states of mind, if persisted in from youth up, grows into a habit which becomes second nature.[46]

Plato would have one of the main aims of the school to be the teaching of goodness. He said, "What advantage can there be in possessing everything except the good, or in understanding everything else while of the good and desirable we know nothing?"[47]

Selectivity and Guidance

The central theme of Plato's educational philosophy revolved around the problem of selection and guidance. It was important that every man in the state he helped in choosing the occupation for which he was best suited. It was more important that the best man was chosen to administer it. The future of the community depended upon its rulers. Plato told us:

> There must be selection. Let us note among the guardians those who in their whole life show the greatest eagerness to do what is for the good of their country, and the greatest repugnance to do what is against her interests. They will have to be watched at every age, in order that we may see whether they preserve their resolution, and never, under the influence either of force or enchantment, forget or cast off their sense of duty to the state.[48]

Selection was based upon character and intelligence—such qualities as gentleness, faithfulness and devotion for advanced education and leadership.

Selection and guidance for the citizens of the state was primarily occupational selection and guidance. It was concerned with every man doing the work for which he was best suited.

This is what Plato meant by justice. He described it in the following passage:

> Further, we affirmed that justice was doing one's own business and not being a busybody; we said so again and again, and many others have said the same to us . . . Then on this view also justice will be admitted to be the having and doing what is a man's own, and belongs to him.[49]

Fundamentally selection was based upon the principles of psychology. Plato erected the first rules by which men and women could be assisted in achieving a high degree of occupational performance. He also set up psychological rules for selecting women for different occupations and for guiding them in all aspects of their life. The rules he used as an aid in guidance were:

1. Selection should depend only upon the psychological aspects of personality which were directly related to a specific occupation, all other personality characteristics were superfluous.
2. Women possessed the same characteristics as men, differed in physical strength only. They had equal rights to education and occupations.
3. All students would profit from a basic education, but after a point some students would no longer profit due to lack of abilities directly related to education. These students could profit from other types of education particularly vocational education.[50]

The last factor Plato set up to be considered in selection and guidance was that of interest. He recognized the fact that a person could have superior abilities but not have an interest in advanced studies.

Plato summarized his stand on selection by stating:

> There are the points which you must consider; those who have most comprehension, and who are more steadfast in their learning, and in their military and other appointed duties, when they have arrived at the age of thirty will have to be chosen by you out of the select class, and elevated to higher honour; and you will have to prove them by the help of

dialectic, in order to learn which of them is able to give up the use of sight and the other senses, and in company with truth to attain absolute being.[51]

Plato's Educational Psychology

Plato was the first writer to present a system of psychology. His theories regarding psychology had certain implications for education.

Plato felt that experiences began in the intra-uterine period. He stated that expectant mothers were to have a peaceful prenatal period and should engage in cultural pursuits. Plato never stated how this could be beneficial.

Plato believed that the psyche was a growing, living, dynamic thing. Thus the training of children in early life, in part, determines their future—for good or for evil. Plato said, "The beginning is always the most important part, especially in dealing with anything young and tender. That is the time when the character is being moulded and easily takes any impression one may wish to stamp on it."[52]

Plato indicated in the *Republic* that the individual personality, as the state, was composed of three parts.[53]

The first or lowest level of personality was the concupiscent.[54] This stage not only implied the desire for erotic outlet, but like the "Id" it was a force or stage which encompassed all the physical desires. It was appetitive, it sought gratification, it resembled the amoeba in that its purpose was controlled by its appetites. This stage does not mean that it was barbaric or primitive. It could develop sophistication. The gourmet who has pressed duck and champagne is basically no different than the fellow who has pig hocks and beer; both are satisfying the appetitive phase of their existence.

This first level may be further broken down to two divisions: (1) the level of good appetites, that is, desires that are good for the body, or which may be developed for the good of the state; and (2) bad appetites, which lead for example to lawlessness, crime, and brutality. The majority of men exist on this concupiscent level and for them Plato has little to say or to offer. The problem is to tame them, to make them fit into society. Justice demands that they be made into useful citizens; this must be done by regulation. A basic weakness of Plato's was that he would regulate the lives of the "lower" classes without their consent. There is a wildness to this concupiscent stage, and it must be soothed and civilized. How?—by harmony and rhythm that have been nurtured and educated.

> The absence of grace, rhythm, harmony is nearly allied to baseness of thought and expression and baseness of character; whereas their presence goes with that moral excellence and self-mastery of which they are the embodiment.[55]

Harmony will rule over this part of the soul, for it is good for the desires to acknowledge the rule of reason. This rule of reason over the strong desires is temperance. "Temperance means a kind of orderliness, a control of certain pleasures and appetites."[56]

The second stage of the soul is that of passion or spirit. Passion is different than desire in that it is related to reason. In the war between reason and desire, passion is on the side of reason.

> We were supposing this spirited element to be something of the nature, of appetite; but now it appears that, when the soul is divided into factions, it is far more ready to be up in arms on the side of reason.[57]

For Plato passion seemed to be a conscience, as it attempted to do good. It was similar to courage for whatever was good for the state, that is, whatever was derived to enhance the institutions of government, was the same as that which enhanced the individual and this quality was courage.

The last stage, and the highest of the three is that of reason. Reason is different from the first two in that it is a love of wisdom. Plato realized that the other two forces were in all men. The wise man satisfied the desires, not too much or too little, but in moderation before he left for the realm of ". . . solitude of pure abstraction, free to contemplate and aspire to the knowledge of the unknown whether in the past, present, or future."[58] This is the realm in which by training and reason one attains the truth.

The goal of the first stage was material gain. The second stage sought honor for its end. This stage always implies pursuit—pursuit of knowledge. Knowledge must be sought after; for if all knowledge were known the possessor would in fact be a god. Man, because of his nature, can only seek after and love knowledge, he never truly possesses it.

In the *Republic* the person who existed on this level was a philosopher. He was not unaware of the previous stages; he had tasted them and rejected them because of the "sweetness of learning and knowing truth." Plato holds that this tasting of the lower levels was good for the philosopher because it gave him experiences and understanding of the problems and conditions of the lower classes.

Plato was emphatic in his belief that the philosopher had the pleasantest life, for the greatest delight is in attaining knowledge, and can only be known by him. The pleasures of knowledge are permanent, while those of the senses are variable and subject to change; this range of intensity produces unhappiness. The philosopher is described as one who loves knowledge or wisdom.

An important consideration is that the philosopher is not only a gatherer of facts, but he lives the "good life," he is not addicted to the "mean" qualities that the two lower classes possess. He lives on a loftier plane.

Plato attempted to simplify and catalog human nature, human needs, and human social life. He proposed a personality triad of psychological elements, and attempted to develop this triad into a system composed of three main personality types. To reduce all humans to three types, and then to relegate these restricted types to specific occupations and positions within the state is an example of Plato's arbitrary attitude toward human rights. However, to attempt a critical study of personality itself was an innovation in the area of psychology.

The *Republic* contained and contributed several ideas to the area of education that have been wholley or in part actualized.

The first major idea related to education was Plato's suggestion of the division of schools into primary, secondary, college, and graduate school. There exists in the United States closer adherence to Plato's plan than is found in the school systems of other countries. However, the spirit of Plato's suggested plan of divisions is followed in all countries, that is, the separation of schools by age, according to students and educational material. For example, the movement toward universal educational systems in Europe has tended to produce schools that correspond to divisions of elementary education, secondary education, college education and graduate school.[59] However, the European school systems do not follow the contemporary American plan of providing twelve years of public schooling, divided into elementary and secondary education.

Platonic idea of compulsory education is becoming actualized impetus, which came about particularly after World War II. Such countries as China, Czechoslovakia, Germany, Japan, Norway, Russia and India have proposed and adopted schemes of compulsory education.

To understand the role of women in Greece is to realize how shocking was Plato's thesis for equality of the sexes in education. Women were in the subordinate position; they were little better than slaves. Plato proposed that women be given educational benefits on a par with male education, and that female education should equip women to accept the highest positions they were capable of attaining both in the government as well as in other occupations. Plato realized that to grant women equal education would raise their status and make them co-equal partners in all endeavors with men. Modern educational philosophy has, in the main, accepted the fact that women should have the same opportunites as men.

Closely allied with Plato's idea of a structured school system was the concept of the educational program under the administration of the government, reserving ultimately certain prerogatives with the people. The countries of Asia, Europe, as well as the United States have followed Plato's suggestion of a public school system under the control of public officials who hold office either through public election or by appointment. In the United States the main direction is given to public schools by reserving most of its control to the local community. However, in other coutries—for example, England and France—the direction is more remote being vested in the central government.

The curriculum, proposed by Plato, was based upon the idea that knowledge of certain subjects—in particular, mathematics including arithmetic and geometry, astronomy, music and logic—would help in the pursuit of truth. The study of the humanities, character education, as well as gymnastics was also suggested by Plato as being important in the intellectual growth of the individual. Plato's proposals were incorporated into the educational programs of the medievalists, and until the renaissance, were the mainstay of the curriculum. Modern educational practices still utilize Plato's proposed classes with the exception of character education, mainly on the university level, and now they are not required classes, as Plato hoped they would be, but are electives.

Summary and Conclusions

The *Republic* was an important contribution to the field of education. While there are inconsistencies and weaknesses in the work, there were also many proposals of value.

In the field of philosophy Plato has made many original contributions. Pertinent to the area of education was his theory of knowledge. Plato felt an intense dislike for opinion; truth must be the goal of the wise man. Truth can be ascertained by using the correct method. Truth resides in the eternal forms. The correct education enables one to know the forms.

The central problem of the *Republic* was the nature of justice. Justice is essentially a harmonious relationship existing within the individual and within the state. Ultimately it is every man performing the job or function to which he is best suited. Psychologically it is the balance of the three levels of the soul, the concupiscent, passion, and the reason level. Education was the means Plato utilized to insure justice.

The whole school program proposed by Plato was set up to give men the techniques to search for and to discover truth. The school was not only charged with giving men a method of inquiry, it was to help them secure justice. In order to insure securing his aims Plato posited a curriculum based upon the study of mathematics, logic, astronomy, and music. Gymnastics were included in the course of studies because Plato believed in developing the body to insure a healthy mind.

Advanced graduate work was offered to those students who were selected after careful consideration. Ultimately the students who spent their life in the pursuit of knowledge, the philosophers, were selected to govern the state.

The *Republic* has certain fundamental problems and contradictions, the two most important being the use of myths, and the nature of democracy in Plato's proposed new state.

Plato was in the main opposed to democracy in that the division of classes he proposed assumed that only the small elite class had the ability to make governmental decisions. Plato stated that ruling is an art similar to shoemaking or medicine. The shoemaker must have the natural abilities and the specialized work. He does not by any stretch of the imagination possess the capacity or educational training required to engage in masonry. Using this theory of specialization Plato said that ruling is also an art, and that unless a man possessed the abilities and training, he could not make wise decisions concerning the administration of the state.

The fundamental thesis of the *Republic* that knowledge and education are beneficial to all the citizens of the state, and that all must partake in a comprehensive and universal school program, is among the most significant of Plato's contributions. After 2,000 years it is still an important message.

chapter three

THE NATURE OF THE CONCEPT IN THE *UTOPIA*

THERE IS A TIME-SPAN of almost 1,800 years between the writing of the *Republic* and the publication of the *Utopia.* During this period of eighteen centuries it appears that the concept of utopia, previously developed by Plato and utilized with the expectation of procuring a change in the social structure, disappeared. The early medieval period produced a form of utopia which was dedicated to the idea of escape—escape from the problems that appeared to be insolvable. St. Augustine, in the *City of God,* placed utopia in the next world. To St. Augustine and to many others, the city of man appeared wicked, a place where many men had developed an attitude of cynicism and "worldliness." Medieval ideology posited a construct which emphasized that the people who rejected the city of man and followed the way of Christ could assuredly expect their reward in the Kingdom of Heaven.

Problems pertaining to social life in England were especially marked. The people during the late medieval period underwent a great deal of suffering and dislocation because of the economic changes that were taking place. This was due to the fact that in England the pattern of capitalism developed first into agriculture and trade and only later and more slowly did it develop into industry. The inevitable consequences of these economic changes resulted in a new class structure. A large proletariat developed. The proletariat were the disinherited. Tenant farming became extinct in England. Wool became a major source of income. A system of enclosures—pastures for sheep—became widespread. The tenant farmers were displaced and unemployed. Widespread unemployment, rapidly rising prices, political and moral corruption, savage repressive laws against the poorer class, and constant wars between states arising out of the breakdown of feudal society characterized the early sixteenth century. There was a general sense of bewilderment and despair. Even that institution which appeared most stable, the universal and undivided Church, was passing, and there seemed nothing to take its place. Related to this decay, however, was the growth of a new class, the merchants. This new bourgeoisie, confident of its growing power, offered stability and order. In order to entrench themselves in the Tudor world the merchants mapped out a new world utilizing internal stability and a secure world market.

This world, characterized by a large class of restless poor, an emerging bourgeoisie, a lessening of Church power, and a change in political philosophy, was the world in which Thomas More grew to manhood. It was a world of conflict and contrast, of despair and hope, of idealism and corruption, of increasing wealth and increasing poverty, and a world of growing nationalism.

More was a member of the merchant class, and as Kautsky pointed out, often its spokesman.[1] His father was a prominent lawyer and later a judge. More himself was a guest for many years in the home of Archbishop Morton, the chief minister of Henry VIII. In spite of his attraction for the life of the scholar, More became a lawyer. He became a member of Parliament, and he also acted as a spokesman for the city of London. Because of his ability he was increasingly called into the service of the crown, and finally in 1529 he became the first layman to be appointed Lord Chancellor. He resigned this office in 1532 because of Henry VIII's church policy. Almost immediately after his resignation he was incarcerated in the Tower, and in July, 1553, he was beheaded on a charge of treason. Certain aspects of More's life will be discussed in greater detail as they are germane to parts of the *Utopia* which will be dealt with later. However, it will be well to say something of his character and intellectual background.

More associated with the ablest and most brilliant men of

the Renaissance age. Among his close acquaintances were John Colet, Thomas Linacre, William Latimer, and Erasmus.[2] More was also a member of the king's family at a time when the greatest minds of England and the Continent graced the English capital.

Many of More's friends had studied in Italy and had come under the influence of those ardent scholars who had devoted their lives to the recovery and study of Greek literature and philosophy. The interest in Greek caused the study of Plato to be revived. It also prompted Erasmus to publish a new Greek translation of the New Testament. Another aspect of this new learning was a revived interest in the Fathers of the Church. More was particularly interested in St. Augustine.

This new learning, collectively called Humanism, though it was an original doctrine, still possessed many of the ideas and terminology of Scholasticism. However, Humanism surpassed the dogma of Scholasticism by rejecting such dogmas as that of original sin and Satan. Humanism substituted the idea that man and the world can be infinitely improved.

The medieval period can be described in part as a time of renunciation. Men looked for an utopia of escape. The contemporary attitude was essentially that this life was wicked and that men must renounce the concupiscent pleasures, arranged by Satan for their downfall. Heaven promised eternal bliss. Men could rationalize the injustice and meanness of their lives by holding to a reward system in the future. However, Humanism refused to accept such a doctrine. Humanism developed a new attitude that stated in effect that this life must be made good. The old beliefs in the idea of Satan and the intrinsic baseness of mankind were replaced with the idea that stated mankind could be improved. Humanism held that the social conditions of men were subject to continuous improvement. Humanism, in the hands of a man like More, proposed happiness for all men, not just a few men in the elite group.

The Humanists were greatly drawn to the study of Greek and Latin. The works of Plato in particular were rediscovered by these sixteenth-century thinkers. The *Republic*, which emphasized justice—which meant the placing of each man in the job for which he was best suited, and the recognition of the rights and duties of each class—was certainly a starting point for More's idea of a model commonwealth. The *Republic* also contained ideas regarding a fixed perfect constitution, an elaborate educational system, and a concept of a religion calculated to serve social stability. These ideas were accepted by More and were incorporated into his *Utopia.* However, More did not accept Plato's ideas per se, merely inserting them in his book. The *Utopia* is a logical, step by step, analysis of the principles upon which the perfect state should be based. One major aspect of More's book which differed from Plato's was that Utopia was a nation not merely a city-state. Another important consideration was that More presented a classless society, whereas Plato felt that justice demanded a stratified community. More realized that no matter how noble the intentions of an elite were there would always be the tendency of the upperclass to oppress the weak majority. This oppression would be intensified if the majority were without property. The problems of property, class, and the relations of the state are the core of the first book of the *Utopia.*

The *Utopia* was written by More in 1515 and was published the following year.[3] The Utopia was divided into two sections. The first section was an analysis of More's contemporary society. The second half of the book described the land of Utopia.

More understood his contemporary world. He paid close attention to the tendencies and conditions that existed during that time; because of this it was possible for More to make predictions concerning the future.

More's Plan for the Improvement of the Human Community

More began his plan for improvement of society by examining the causes of the development of social classes, the growing poverty of the propertyless citizens, and the problems of decay within the Church.

The first point discussed by More concerned the inequalities of the English economic system. From what More said in the *Utopia* it would appear that the crime rate, particularly in the area of thievery, was high in contemporary England. A large segment of the lower class, the tenant farmers, were dispossessed from their lands through the policy of enclosures. These tenant farmers were unable to locate employment; hence, they turned to stealing. In spite of the almost daily hangings of thieves, men continued to steal in order to eat. The situation was analyzed by More:

> Great and horrible punishments are appointed for thieves, whereas much rather provision should have been made that there were some means whereby they might get their living, so that no man should be driven to this extreme necessity, first to steal and then to die for it.[4]

Labor was displaced also by creating new labor-saving devices. Decreased wages, displaced labor, plus increased profits for the wealthy elite produced misery and discontent for the great mass of English citizens.

The small wealthy upper class of More's England lived in great luxury. More said that "... the unreasonable covetousness of a few hath been the undoing of England."[5] The wealthy class had lost all contact with the poor people. The precepts of Christian charity, which More held dear, were ignored by the moneyed elite. Ostentatious display and a morbid concern with pleasure were part of the life of the upperclass.[6]

In order to bring human happiness and social justice into human society More offered several proposals in the *Utopia*.

The abolition of property was his first proposal. In order to promote a classless society and the equality of all citizens, More intended his society to be based upon a form of communism, which included abolition of private property and the establishment of common possession of all commodities.[7] More believed that the problem of crime, poverty, and class hostility would be eradicated. However, More was overly idealistic in assuming that all men would renounce their natural impulses in individual matters in order to promote the aims of the whole society.

Plato's communism influenced More, but there are several evident differences between Platonic communism and Utopian communism in the application of principles. In the *Republic* only the soldiers and the guardians lived a communal life, while in the *Utopia* all the people followed a communal existence. In the former the soldiers and guardians were exempt from manual labor. This was not true in Utopia, where all citizens were craftsmen. In Plato's proposed state the government was aristocratic, but in Utopia the government had strong democratic aspects.

More based his ideas of the promotion of the public weal upon the elimination of desire. The Utopians were taught to disdain material possessions. For example, since money was not needed in a communistic economy,[8] gold was considered inferior to iron. In Utopia children's playthings were made of gold, and an adult who used gold as an ornament would be considered retrogressive.

The anti-materialistic society of More was perhaps carried to extreme, for example, in the matter of dress. More felt that dress was a matter of class cleavage and dissensions. All of the citizens of Utopia wore similar garments made of white wool, the only difference being the design, one type for women and another type for men.

Another aspect of More's forced social-relationships was the common dining halls. There can be little criticism of the efficacy of taking meals in common; it would save duplication, time, and resolve many kindred problems. More appeared to be more interested, however, in the fact that eating together would produce, primarily, cultural results. It was a means of inculcating morals, spurring discussions, developing character and generally lifting the cultural level.[9]

More imbued the *Utopia* with the idea that there should never be any personal rivalry in the new state. Individuals were never compared. Each person was protected by the state and encouraged to develop along his own lines of interest and abilities.

The second proposal of More, a democratic form of government, contained elements of autocracy. This was undoubtedly due to his own position in the English hierarchy, but it was also based upon his interest in behavioral engineering.[10] More was naively unaware that his Utopian government could under the wrong auspices degenerate into a form of benevolent absolutism which would in turn crush individual opportunity. More attempted to balance a paternalistic government with democracy by requiring a representative assembly and, at certain times, voting by all citizens. An example of the paternalism of the state was the control of marriage and reproduction. More felt that child bearing and rearing were too important to be left to the whims of individuals. More appeared to have had little faith and trust in people, for example, he wanted the child to identify with the group, to feel a genuine affection for all, and not for just his parents, who might actually harm his personality because of personal eccentricities. The main task of the government was to provide a social climate in which equal opportunity could exist. There was, in Utopia, no organized mediocrity to hold back the good. Spontaneity was encouraged. Each person was permitted much freedom of development. What rank did exist in Utopia was based upon intellectual attainments. The governmental leaders, as in the *Republic*, were men chosen because of their superior knowledge. More naively assumed that once the state was established along his proposed lines the government would have little function.

The third proposal was concerned with religious belief. The *Utopia* was committed to the idea of religious toleration. Any person could believe in religion or choose to deny religion, according to his conscience. However, the majority of Utopians followed a specific religion. This religion was completely rationalistic. This is a reflection of More's whole attitude, for the ideal state was based upon reason alone; it was a philosophical city. Both Plato and More agreed in employing only reason to arrive at fundamentals. There were no religious truths arrived at in the Utopia by revelation. It is conceivable that More's rationalistic religion was a criticism of Catholic England. The *Utopia* could have been in part an attempt to shame the Christians of the sixteenth century by showing what an ideal state pagans could produce by reason alone.[11]

The last proposal, and the one with which More was most concerned, was education.

The Educational Program

More's educational philosophy is part of a unified whole. The central doctrine of the *Utopia* was a praise of pleasure.[12] More said that pleasure was good and honest in itself. Since pleasure[13] or happiness resided only in what is good and honest it must not involve the loss of a greater pleasure,[14] consequent pain or sorrow, or injury to one's neighbor, as for example in portioning out the commodities of life.[16] The norm for what is good lay in what is natural; for example, the previously stated Utopian disdain for gold was based upon the fact that gold of its own nature was a thing unprofitable to man, for nature has given to gold no special use without which man cannot easily survive.

More lauded certain forms of bodily pleasure. In this category he included a controlled form of sense pleasure and a state of physical well-being or health. The *Utopia* contained many references to hygiene. For example, the Utopians had hospitals, utilized quarantine,[17] controlled diet, and required healthful, clean conditions in the city.[18]

The chief pleasures for More, however, were the pleasures of the soul. The first of these pleasures was the self-rewarding exercise of virtue. Virtue was defined as ". . . a life ordered according to nature, and that we be hereunto [sic] ordained of God. And that following the course of nature, is ruled thus by reason."[19] Living a virtuous life would lead to true happiness, More said, for the rewards were a serene consciousness of one's own moral excellence, a happy memory of one's conduct in the past and an unshakable hope for bliss in the future.[20] More did not demand that one disassociate himself from the community or from comfort to lead the good life. He said:

> A virtuous life is a joyful life for when nature biddeth thee to be good and gentle to others she commandeth thee not to be cruel and ungentle to thyself.[21]

The second great pleasure of the soul comes from learning.[22] Learning was the most important activity in the *Utopia*. More said that good citizens, those who had contempt for false pleasures and who loved true pleasures, were formed "partly by education and partly by good literature and learning."[23] More did not indicate what the difference between education and learning was; it would appear that the distinction was not important to him. What More meant by education would probably be termed informal education today, and learning or formal education would be under the auspices of a regular school.

One main reason for More's concern with education was that the *Utopia* was to a large extent More's appraisal and criticism of contemporary Scholastic education. More, as well as Andreae, Campanella, and Bacon, found Scholasticism distasteful. More's criticism of Scholasticism expressed itself in a condemnation of the dialectical sophistry and subtle disputations of the Scholastics. In the *Utopia* More said:

> The Utopians have not devised one of all those rules of restrictions, amplifications, and suppositions, very wittily invented in the small logicals which in Europe our children in every place do learn.[24]

Added to this, More also stated, "But as the Utopians are in all things they be almost equal to our old ancient writers, so our present Utopian scholars and logicians in subtle inventions have far passed and gone beyond them."[25]

These two quotations taken together indicate that More equated the Utopian's development of logic with that of the Greek philosophers, and in particular Aristotle. More wanted to exclude the use of the innumerable medieval commentaries and accretions that made up a large part of the study of logic and philosophy in the schools of More's contemporary England and on the Continent. He wanted the Utopian schools to utilize the works of the early Greek writers. He seems to have wanted none of the Scholastic teachings of logic in Utopian schools which were based upon the small logicals.[26] The students in the schools of More's contemporaries were required to commit the small logicals to memory even though they did not understand them. Having taken the course of studies in logic during his school days, More found the memorization of the small logicals particularly distasteful.

He felt that the reform schools proposed in the *Utopia* had to get away from the subtle inventions of the Scholastics (as particularly evidenced in the small logicals) and had to return to Aristotle in whose works there was an instrument sufficient to meet and solve the problems of intellectual life. More was perhaps the leading advocate of the return to the Greek writers, but he received the complete support of his fellow Humanists. Such men as Erasmus and John Colet, close friends of More, were exponents of the return to the Greeks.[27]

The success of any program of educational reform rests upon the attitude of the citizens toward it. More's solution to this problem was to involve virtually every citizen of Utopia in education. The Utopians felt that learning was man's greatest pleasure. More described it in this manner:

> The citizens spend few hours in work, they withdraw from bodily service to the free liberty of the mind and the garnishing of the same. For herein they suppose the happiness of this life to consist.[28]

The citizens of Utopia committed themselves to the proposition that learning was fundamental to happiness and pleasure. Thus it became necessary for More to arrange the school system, so that they could participate. The students were divided into three classes: (1) all children of school age (since education was compulsory and universal in Utopia),[29] (2) a few talented persons, scholars by profession, who were free from work to devote themselves exclusively to study,[30] and (3) a large part of the population, which devoted part of each day to education.[31]

The Curriculum of the Schools in Utopia

More began his discussion of the curriculum of Utopian schools by proposing a program of classics. The classics for More meant almost exclusively the literature of Greece.[32]

On the one hand More's espousal of the Greek books was a positive contribution in the area of educational reform. However, it appeared to be More's main contribution to the content of learning, at least for those students—the scholars and adults—for whom he stated that learning was the most precious aspect of their lives. Certainly More's idea that education must be engaged in by the majority of the population, is a sound idea, but it is another thing to propose a curriculum to fit the needs of all adults, a curriculum which More neglected. He undoubtedly felt that cultural enrichment was an important aspect of education and that the Greek books offered, among other things, the best source for cultural education. However, it was naive of More to assume that all students would find the desire or interest to spend a large part of their day pursuing the Greek classics. Further, More never substantiated his doctrine that the Greek books would provide all the citizens with an instrument sufficient to meet and solve the intellectual problems of life.

More began his list of Greek books with the philosophers Plato and Aristotle. Plato was an important force in Renaissance philosophy. His influence was unsurpassed even by Aristotle.[33] The Humanists were particularly indebted to Plato. More's obligation to Plato was particularly great. The idea of the *Utopia* as well as some of the particulars contained in it came from the *Republic*.

Certain factors must be taken into consideration when considering the fact that More proposed the erecting of a curriculum on Plato's works. Four centuries separate us from More's period. One of the difficulties in trying to understand a past era is the effort needed to forget the changes in thought that have taken place between that period and our own. In an attempt to reach an approximate appreciation on More's point of view of regarding Aristotle as inferior to Plato, we must attempt to obliterate the influence of Aristotle in the intervening centuries.[34] More indicated in the Utopia that the works of Plato were the most important and Aristotle's works were placed in a subordinate position in the list of Greek books. The fact that Aristotle was unappreciated by More, and by the Humanists in general, was probably because Aristotle was the god of the Scholastics. Another point to be considered was that More and his fellow Humanists were in revolt against the shoddy Latin found in the schools, the Church, and in all books published during the sixteenth century. In the *Utopia* More expressly forbade any Latin in the schools.[35] The Latin translations of

Aristotle that More saw and that influenced him so strongly were inferior because the Latin was poor and because the works were incomplete. More stressed the point that no translation was as good in regards to influence and style as the original Greek. His insistence on including only the Greek books in his program shows that by 1515 the Humanists felt that in Greek writing one could find all that was worth knowing and preserving. More, in keeping with the spirit of the Renaissance, was demanding a return to the primary sources.[36]

There is a contradiction in More's statement that all learning took place in the vernacular, for he emphasized the study of Greek. He gave no adequate reasons for his insistence of Greek studies. There is no mention in the *Utopia* of the Greek books being translated. Contrariwise there is evidence that the Utopians held the study of Greek in great esteem, for More said:

> When the Utopians heard me speak of the Greek literature of learning they made earnest suit unto me that I would teach and instruct them in that tongue and learning. Therefore in less than three years space there was nothing in the Greek tongue that they lacked.[37]

More did not state whether all the citizens studied Greek or whether it was included in the schools. However, More wanted all the citizens to study the Greek classics. A basic inconsistency existed, which More did not resolve: it concerned the improbability of the student's ability to read the classics without a knowledge of Greek.

More stated that the poetical works of Aristophanes, Homer, Erupides and Sophocles would be included in the list of Greek classics. The books of Thucydides, Herodotus and Herodian were a component of the history section. In the area of science Hippocrates' and Galen's works in medicine were included as well as Theophrastus' work involving plants. This list of Greek books was the sum total of the classic literature More meant to include in his educational reforms. It was a meager list for a program of advanced education.

The utopian writers did not write books or propose schemes that were tangential departures from the social base. More, as well as the other utopists, attempted in his utopia to suggest a method for the introduction of new ideas and elements into social life. These ideas would require new and different ways of living. More's luxuriant imagination produced many novel ideas, but he realized that in order to get the support of society he could not disturb society too deeply, or reject all that was good in social life merely beacuse it was traditional. Thus, the backbone of the curriculum of the schools of Utopia remained the quadrivium.[38]

The only course that More appeared to be concerned with enough to discuss in any detail was logic.[39] As has already been indicated More wanted a return to the logic contained in the works of Aristotle. Fundamentally More wanted to subordinate subtlety to utility in the area of logic.

In summary, More felt that by returning to a study of classical science and knowledge the Utopians could release themselves from the sterile preoccupation the European thinkers had with dialectic and universals. Of course, More weighted the argument in favor of the Utopia by making it, unlike Europe, a non-Christian country. Thus the Utopians were not forced to reconcile pagan authors with Christianity. For example, while the Church frowned upon scientific research the Utopians were committed to scientific investigation. In fact the Utopians penetrated into the mysteries of nature. More said, "The Utopians think that the contemplation of nature and the praise thereof is to God a very acceptable honor."[40] Thus, in part, the *Utopia* was a plea to widen and to extend the frontiers of scientific and all knowledge and the first step was to master classical Greek science.

Educational Opportunities for Women

The idea that women should have equal rights and privileges was commonly held by the utopists. More followed Plato by proposing that women should have equal opportunity in the area of education and politics. More felt as Campanella did that women should become priests provided that they were qualified.[41]

Education was compulsory for both sexes in the Utopian primary and secondary schools. More said, "All of their children are instructed in learning,"[42] and again More stated, "Both childhood and youth are instructed and taught of them."[43] A two year term at the farm was required after the completion of secondary school, after which time women who qualified were allowed to attend the schools of higher learning. Eventually those women who showed aptitude for studies were allowed to join one of the highest ranks in the state, the rank of teacher-priest.

The equality of women was qualified. More offered women the possibility of holding various offices, but he limited the number of women who could hold the office, and he raised an extremely difficult requirement:

> "The Priests are men," said More, "except they be women for that kind is not excluded from the priesthood, howbeit few be chosen, and none but widows and old women."[44]

In the elementary and secondary school, girls took the same course of studies as the boys.

More must be given credit for being among the first in proposing equality for women in social life. And even though the equality proposed by More was in a qualified and limited form, nevertheless it was a new and startling concept for a sixteenth-century bourgeoise leader.

More could not entirely release himself from the bonds of sixteenth-century religious and social views regarding the role of women. In the *Utopia* the primary role of women was described as that of wife and mother. Thus More proposed that women would take a great deal of course work in the area of homemaking. The occupational choice of women tended to be restricted primarily to sewing, cooking, and tending young children. However, the fact that More said women had equal opportunity to attend school was an important contribution to social progress.

Character Education in Utopian Schools

When More proposed a program of educational reform he was determined to include a course in character education in the curriculum. He wrote:

> The wholesome and virtuous opinions wherein they were brought up even from their childhood, partly through learning and partly through the ordinances and laws of their weal-public, augment and increase their courage.[45]

More did not, however, state what the content or method of the courses in character education would be. It is possible to infer what More felt good character and right behavior should be from his statements concerning virtue.

More rejected any attempt to develop a system of virtue that would have been a radical departure from the Christian community of which he was a member. Thus, he stated that the Utopian system of ethics was the same as that of contemporary sixteenth-century England. He said, "In that part of philosophy which entreateth of manners and virtue their reasons and opinions agree with ours,"[46] (e.g., England). Moreover, More stated that the Utopians arrived at the proofs for their moral system not through revelation, but by means of reason. He explained, "The principles of the Utopian system of values, morals and religion are believed and granted by proofs of reason."[47] More used a rationalistic basis in selecting a guide for character development and arrived at a simple rule for virtuous conduct—". . . virtue is a life ordered according to nature."[48] More hoped that people would further be motivated to secure the same joy and happiness for other men once they had secured their own happiness.[49] Just how this could be accomplished More did not disclose.

More attempted to create a program of character education without the sanctions of religion. He listed a moral code, but he gave no philosophical basis to substantiate it. The list forbade suicide, premarital sexual relations, stealing, lying, adultery, divorce, disobedience to superiors, intolerance and sloth.

The *Utopia* has reference to some devices for promoting character development apart from the courses in the schools. These devices included statues of people who were noted for piety and these replicas were placed throughout the city.[50] Games were played by the Utopian children that were devised to indicate a moral lesson. Through the participation in games the children were supposed to draw the moral of unity and accord versus disunity and disharmony and good versus evil. Another technique was utilized at the common dining room where ". . . the Utopians begin every dinner and supper with readings that pertain to good manners and virtue."[51]

More's proposal regarding character education was handicapped by several limitations. The failure to define exactly of what character education should consist and how it should be taught are the most outstanding. However, up to the time of the writing of the *Utopia* character education was the province of the priests who performed as teachers of character education with the absolute sanctions of the Church. The fact that More proposed to his contemporaries that character education should become part of the curriculum of a secular system of education was a highly novel proposal.

Adult Education in Utopia

The unity of More's ideas and the integration of his educational reforms into the over-all plan for social, political and economic change are best seen in the area of adult education. The *Utopia* contained the suggestion that the vast majority of the citizens should spend part of each day in educational pursuits.

More proposed an economic basis for Utopian society that would permit each citizen a maximum of leisure time to spend in cultural and educational pursuits.[52] The social life of the state revolved about the school.[53]

Moreover, cultural and educational experiences were incorporated into the daily life of the Utopians through means other than formal techniques embodied in the schools. For example, during the common meals persons were selected to read from various books; afterwards, the readings were discussed by the elders with the young people contributing their ideas.[54] Musical renditions were heard after every dinner for the purpose of improving musical appreciation among the citizens.[55] More did not indicate how effective this technique was, but it would appear that this was another example of More's naivete, for he held the fundamental tenet that merely exposing people to art, culture, and knowledge would make them devotees. He did not adequately reason out the problem of motivation in educational pursuits. The fact that he did not do this weakens his arguments.

The average day of the vast majority of the Utopians began by attending one of the many lectures that were offered.[56] The Utopians attended the lectures according to individual preference. No restrictions were made in regard to attendance, tests, or credits. It appears that people attended the lectures for the sheer joy of learning. More appeared to believe that people would participate in learning activities for the pleasure of learning.

Vocational Education in More's Utopia

More's idea of what the role of education should be in the lives of the Utopians was consistent. He felt that the school should provide courses which, to a large degree, were designed to furnish each student with the theory and practical experiences required, in part, to master a specific occupation.

All the students of Utopia learned a minimum of two trades. The first trade in which each and every student was required to become proficient, was agriculture.

> "Husbandry is a science common to them all," More said, "both men and women. In this they be all instructed even from their youth, partly in their schools, and partly in the country."[57]

More had several reasons for requiring all the students to take the academic course in agriculture which included an apprentice program. One reason was economic.[58] During harvest time most of the citizens, except those excused because of their studies or because of their health, went to the farms and assisted in the farm work.[59] The two years of farm work required of each student in the agriculture apprentice program also supplied a continuous source of workers on the large state-owned farms.

Another reason for More's insistence upon students knowing the fundamentals of agriculture was not directly related to large-scale farming itself. More felt that people would develop a spiritual sense by working the soil, raising crops, (both vegetable and floral), and by seeing the rhythm in the cycle of seasons, and they would satisfy a deeply felt need to be at one with nature. From this appreciation of nature, More argued, people would become close to the God of nature.

Every adult in Utopia had a private garden. The citizens' gardens were located between the houses. The gardens contained some vegetables and many flowers. Utopian families spent part of each day in their gardens. This activity was very important, according to More, for it supplied not only a sense of creative activity, but enabled the Utopians to profit by exercise, relaxation, and recreation as well. It also gave the family an opportunity to engage in an activity together since they spent so much of their time with the community.

One area of interest to the Utopians, but which negated More's idea of communal living was the interest in private gardens. More said that ". . . Utopians set great store by their gardens."[60] The family pride in the garden was further abetted by the competition between families, and by competition between neighborhoods and even cities. These gardens were one of the major pleasures of the Utopians.[61] More said:

> Truly you shall not lightly find in all the city anything that is more commodious than their gardens, either for the profit of the citizens or for pleasure. Therefore it may seem that the first founder of the city minded nothing so much as these gardens.[62]

It is the writer's thesis that many utopian educational proposals have been injected into the mainstream of present day educational philosophy and practice and many of More's educational ideas are found in practice today. The principal institution in the state of Utopia was a well-defined and elaborate school system. More's concept of a school system directed by a department within the government devoted to education, and divided into elementary, secondary, college and adult education levels has been realized in most of the western world.[63] The development of this particular practice began in America in the early part of the last century.[64]

Compulsory education, which More felt was important, is now

accepted in the United States[65] and in many parts of the world, for example, in England, France, Germany and Italy.[66]

Education presented in the vernacular was a concept proposed in the *Utopia* and is accepted today. More believed in the most efficient utilization of the available resources of men and materials, thus vocational education was a major technique used in the schools to equip men with skills that utilized their abilities. Today vocational education is a part of many school systems in the United States as well as in many foreign countries.[67] For example, the following countries among others have occupational training programs: Canada,[68] Germany[69] and Italy.[70]

Science, for More and the other utopists, was a vital part of the curriculum because it was one of the chief means of exploitation of the natural resources. Science is also an important part of the modern school system in America as well as in the rest of the world.[71] The years following World War II have produced an increased awareness of the importance of the sciences, but perhaps the greatest impetus came in 1957 with the launching of the first earth satellite by Russia. America now gives financial encouragement to schools offering science courses and to students specializing in the sciences, particularly on the university level.

In the United States some of More's educational ideas have not been accepted[72] and among the major ideas are: More's suggestions of extensive adult education and free colleges.

To a large degree an extensive system of continuing adult education (which would be possible in a small polis as More envisaged), will be difficult to establish in the United States. One reason for this lies in the size of the American population and the extent of her land area, coupled with the diversity of occupations. These factors preclude the possibility of assembling people, (as they were assembled in the *Utopia* in common halls) for the purpose of education. However, the philosophy of adult education as suggested in part by More, may be to a large degree realized by developing a positive attitude regarding the worth of education and by using various techniques, for example, extensive use of television and radio. It is now possible in many cities for adults to secure the first two years of college in their homes by taking a television course sponsored by local colleges, but in the main the audience consists of curious adults watching the program to satisfy, in part, a need for continuing education. Many public service and educational programs are scheduled on television and radio and are financed by such organizations as the Ford Foundation. Some informal techniques[73] might be tried also and one means may be, for example, the creation of a Federal television station that would utilize exclusively cultural, educational and experimental presentations.

The idea of free university training for the more able student has not gained public acceptance to date. There is, however, a trend among some institutions toward free college education. Many junior colleges offer free tuition to resident students, as do the junior colleges of California. Congress granted loans in 1958 for those students majoring in the sciences and in teaching. It is doubtful, however, that free college education will ever become universal. A careful study should be made to discover the attitude of Americans toward this question. Perhaps the majority of citizens would not be in favor of free college education.

Limitations of the Utopia, Summary and Conclusions

Thomas More has proposed a reform state that was, in the main, ascetic and primitive. Utopia was a country erected upon the concepts of social justice, communal property, the use of the scientific exploitation of natural resources and the value of education.

Many of More's ideas were original. They were the product of a fertile imagination and they transcended his time. However, More was a product of his era and thus possessed many of the intellectual limitations of his time. No man can perceive all the social changes that will develop, but a social reformer should be able to anticipate some of the changes and incorporate provisions regarding them. More's *Utopia* suffered from many weakness, due in part to his failure in adequately perceiving the unfolding of social processes, and in part due to his limited view.

More spoke highly of freedom in the *Utopia,* but nevertheless it would be difficult to attain freedom under the social, economic and political conditions he proposed. The opportunity to make choices was limited. For example, the children had virtually no freedom in the schools as regards choosing their own curriculum.[74] The children followed the set curriculum of the quadrivium. There was a lack of variety of course offerings to meet the interests of the pupils. In point of fact, conformity was prized among the Utopians. All the citizens wore exactly the same attire, undistinguished by design, color, or ornamentation. Occupations were few in number and most citizens were relegated to agricultural pursuits. Political choice was limited, as it was in the *Republic,* to the selection of governmental office only by members of the small rank of scholars. Choices for marriage partners were also limited by the state. More was handicapped by being unable to differentiate between what he wanted human beings to be and what they actually could be. Thus another limitation of More's work was an inadequate concept of human nature. More felt that the imperfections of human life stemmed from an improper society and not from human nature itself. By creating the right society More felt that human happiness was possible. He failed to perceive the role of the human mind and spirit in the role of creating the right type of social environment. More also failed to recognize that there were certain personality traits, related in part to intelligence, that are virtually impossible to overcome. These traits include the desire for ownership, privacy, and choice. Further there apepar to be some individuals who are not amenable to social codes and mores, and More does not indicate how these persons would be integrated into his society.

More failed to comprehend the basic laws of learning. He left out all provisions for interest and motivation. He also failed to present a discussion as to the situation most propitious to learning, such as the type of school buildings, the use of audio-visual materials, and the nature of the program of instruction which he would include in his educational program.

More failed to understand the fact that life is a constant

struggle and probably always will contain some type of struggle. Life cannot be completely planned. Accidents occur which create conditions in which men survive or fail. More proposed a social order in which all struggle was eliminated, every want was satisfied. More failed to realize the moral struggle, he did not see that merely removing temptation would not necessarily produce good people. There must be alternatives before there can be freedom and good men are produced by making the right choices, with of course the proper foundation in character education.

A major error of the *Utopia* was the presenting of the reform state as a going concern. More felt that his *Utopia* was the ultimate in social speculation. More found it difficult if not impossible to conceive of progress beyond his projected state. He felt that a perfect unchanging state was possible. More did not realize that a state of social perfection, forever fixed, was impossible. Perhaps More was too generously endowed with the idea that anything, including perfection, was possible if people only willed it. He did not see that Utopia is a state of mind and not a social state.

Albeit the *Utopia* possessed several limitations it did contain much of value. The important contributions to the history of mankind were many. Among More's contribution to the development of the concept of utopia were his ideas advocating the equality of the sexes. While More recognized biological differences between the sexes and made provisions and allowances for them he also was aware of the fact that half of the population could not be placed in an inferior role regarding social, political and educational opportunities. More saw clearly that the economic situation could be realized only when every person, regardless of station in life or of sex, participated in the economic life of the state by working. It was possible to limit the work-day by engaging women in the economic order along with the men.

Religious toleration was advocated by More. He was able to rise above his times by proposing freedom of belief and of conscience. The idea that the physical environment could be controlled was contained in the *Utopia.* More presented the idea that man and nature could be exploited for the best interests of society. The exploitation followed definite rules laid down in the *Utopia.* In the area of health More advocated preventive medicine and eugenics. More was very concerned with diet and exercise and felt that human health would be improved by controlled diet. He felt that common dining halls would benefit man through scientific controlled diets.

chapter four

THE NATURE OF THE CONCEPT IN THE *CITY OF THE SUN*

TOMMASO CAMPANELLA was born in Italy in 1568 of poor and illiterate parents. He died in 1639. When he was fourteen he joined the order of Dominicans. Young Campanella was influenced by Telesio who was an advocate of experimental philosophy. Campanella developed a philosophical system that was in the main rationalistic. He refused to accept Thomistic philosophy, which he felt was based upon authority rather than upon logical proofs.

Campanella's beliefs brought strong opposition from the Church and in 1593 he was sent to prison for heresy. He was released in 1629 by Pope Urban VIII, and returned to Rome where he actively campaigned for a return to the principles of primitive Christianity. He firmly hoped that the Catholic Church would become naturalistic-rationalistic.[1] He felt that the Jews, Protestants, and Moslems could be won for the Faith by dint of argument and proposed a plan whereby Spain and later France could erect a universal theocratic state based upon a renovated Catholic Church.

Tommaso Campanella wrote over one hundred books,[2] mainly in the area of philosophy, but the best known work is his *City of the Sun*.

Plan for the Improvement of the Human Community

The *City of the Sun* contained the idea that the state was primarily an educational institution and it was controlled by an intellectual aristocracy of learning. Campanella followed the tradition which Plato and More originated which made teachers the rulers of the state.

The reform state proposed by Campanella was essentially communal. His philosophy for the new state rested upon the supposition that whatever was good for the state would be good for the people. The people forfeited certain individual rights and in return they received a high material standard of living. The morality behind the exchange of individual choice and freedom for material security was not debated by Campanella. He obviously assumed that the idea of exchanging liberty for concrete security was highly academic in view of the material poverty of his time.

The primary aspect of communal life in the *City of the Sun* was the elimination of all privately owned property. Campanella felt that private ownership of property was a disturbing element in personal and social relationships. He believed that the disruptive effect of privately owned property upon social solidarity could be eliminated only by means of communism.

The philosophical basis for the abolition of private property rested upon the supposition that privately owned possessions begot selfishness,[3] while elimination of selfishness would produce love for the whole community.[4]

Material goods were distributed on an equal basis. Every person received what he needed. "The citizens in the City of the Sun get whatever they need from the community, and no one is denied anything he needs."[5] In order to receive more than the minimum of material needs, however, the citizen had to demonstrate devotion to the state. Rewards were reserved for those who sacrificed all individual goals and desires and devoted themselves to promoting the good of the state.

Campanella proposed a pattern of heterosexual social life that was in the main similar to the plan proposed by Plato. Marriage was a threat to the whole community since it implied private possession. Campanella eliminated marriage in his proposed state and substituted the community of women.[6]

Even though the citizens of the City of the Sun regarded women as common property, licentiousness was not permitted. Campanella wrote:

> The inhabitants of the City of the Sun had their women in common as regards both obedience and bed, but not at any and every time as is the case of beasts, that mate with whatever female is available, rather they do it only by permission and as a matter of procreation.[7]

Campanella felt that human reproduction was the concern of the state. In fact genetics was an advanced science in the City of the Sun. "The noble art of breeding is held in the highest esteem among them."[8] The magistrates were experts in genetics and they decided which of the citizens of the City of the Sun could mate and with whom.

The politics of the *City of the Sun* possessed non-democratic elements. In a democracy the state is actually the servant of the individual, but in Campanella's utopia the individual existed for the state, for example, in the aforementioned area of marriage and reproduction Campanella said:

> The begetting of offspring is managed for the good of the state and not of individuals. The magistrates must be obeyed.[9]

Campanella was either unaware of basic psychological factors underlying the emotions of love and the drive for possessiveness, or he refused to admit them in order to promote an absolute state. Campanella created a monolithic state in order to produce the goods and benefits needed to insure the greatest good for the greatest number.[10]

Campanella believed first of all that artificial constructs regarding rank and privilege should be eliminated.[11] He hoped to accomplish this in the main by two methods: (1) material necessities basic to life and all social activities were held in common,[12] and (2) promotion was gained only by merit and ability. Campanella described the life of the citizens in the following quotation.

> Communal life makes all at the same time rich and poor; rich since they have everything, poor since they own nothing. At the same time they are not slaves to things; rather, things serve them.[13]

Individuals considered for promotion in the City of the Sun were required to have superior intelligence, education and character.[14] Women as well as men could aspire to the advanced governmental positions. Campanella listed the qualifications for promotion as follows: the individuals were required to be learned in several trades and skills, in the natural sciences, in history, law, astronomy, physics, mathematics, agriculture, and philosophy.

In the City of the Sun high standards of health, diet, cleanliness and safety were established.[15] For example, one of the major reasons for Campanella's insistence upon regulated birth control was to insure that the best, e.g., the healthiest children, would be produced. All meals were eaten in common and the food was prepared and supervised by dieticians and physicians. Cleanliness was very important. Campanella stated:

> Great stress is placed upon cleanliness in the streets, in the living quarters, in utensils, in clothing, in the workshops, and in the warehouses.[16]

Political and intellectual freedom was fostered in the City of the Sun. Campanella said, "The citizens engage in constant and eager disputation and argument with one another."[17]

The political philosophy of Campanella was based upon a form of representative democracy. Campanella followed closely the plan of government advocated by More and predated Rousseau's *Social Contract*. Every citizen in the City of the Sun had the right to criticize the governmental leaders and their policies. Campanella described it in this manner:

> At every new moon and every full moon they call a council. All who are twenty years or more are admitted to it. Each one is asked to tell what is wanting in the state, which migistrates are carrying out their duties well and which badly.[18]

In addition to the general bi-monthly councils there were great councils held by the magistrates.[19] Each magistrate was elected to represent a hundred citizens.[20] The magistrates in turn elected the ruler and the heads of the three main divisions of the government: (1) the department of education, genetics, clothing and food, (2) the department of military affairs, and (3) the department governing the sciences.[21] The rulers and the three division leaders ". . . meet every day and they correct, confirm, and execute matters which were decided at the general councils."[22]

The magistrates were elected for various terms, but the ruler and the three department heads, once elected, stayed in office for life. Campanella naively described the rule in relation to the method of replacing the men in the top four offices as:

> The first four will give up their office when one is found who is wiser, more gifted, and purer than themselves. They are so sensible and honorable that they gladly yield to a wiser man and learn from him.[23]

Campanella failed to take into consideration the way human nature[24] was in actuality; he romanticized human nature to the detriment of his political ideals.

Campanella has written a utopia whose main purpose was to propose a form of social life that would give to each person a most hygienic, cultural and secure life. Leisure was spent in cultural and educational pursuits. Every individual's personal comfort and health was the concern of the state. Possibly the most important aspect of Campanella's utopia is the fact that he considered the state as primarily an educational institution.

Educational Philosophy in the City of the Sun

Campanella, as a representative of utopian thought, considered education to be the most important single institution within the state. The ruler of the City of the Sun was euphemistically named "Metaphysic."[25] The three assistants who were also heads of the three main governmental agencies were called "Power," "Wisdom," and "Love," a direct substitution for the theological Trinity.

The chief goal of the people was to ". . . lead a philosophic life in common."[26] Thus, Campanella described the life of the citizens of the City of the Sun:

> In the City of the Sun each one has to work barely four hours a day. The rest of the time is spent in pleasant learning, debating, reading, storytelling, writing, walking, and exercising of mind and body.[27]

Campanella's pedagogical aims must be considered in terms of his goal for education which was to produce cultured, civilized people. Moreover, Campanella realized that an educational philosophy which emphasized the humanities to the exclusion of the practical problems of life would be sterile.[26] Campanella felt strongly that in order to provide for the whole man the schools must of necessity include courses in vocational training.

The school system was a projection of Campanella's social and moral philosophy. Campanella felt that the schools would produce an enlightened citizenry who would have learned the techniques required to live together in a harmonious and ethical society.

Education in the City of the Sun began at the age of one year. All the children between the age of one and three were placed in groups under the supervision of a teacher. The next division of education was composed of all children between the ages of three and seven. At the age of seven the student entered the formal phase of education. This phase continued until the student graduated.

Those students who possessed academic ability and aptitude continued their education at the universities after they completed the secondary school. Those students who were not engaged in formal university education could choose to continue their vocational education at training centers which were located in each city.

Virtually all adults attended lectures each day. The lectures took place in special halls, laboratories, or in the botanical gardens. As in More's Utopia the citizens of the City of the Sun heard educational readings during their principal meals, and musical renditions were given at the close of the mealtime.

A system of rewards was set up to encourage students to perform to the best of their abilities. The rewards contained two elements: (1) appeal to the senses and appetite, and (2) social recognition. Every evening at the meals those students who, in the opinion of the teachers, had performed well during the class periods, were praised by the elders, and further the diligent students received extra portions of food and delicacies. Campanella was emphatic in stressing the fact that the rewards were not exclusively delivered only to the bright students. Intelligence was not the determining factor in judging the issuing rewards; the student who tried the hardest was also considered in the awarding of honors.[29]

One facet of the school system that facilitated education according to Campanella's belief was the fact that all students lived in dormitories located along the sides of the schools.[30] This would mean that the students would be under the complete control of the teachers.

Campanella's theories regarding schools included pre-school training, the full utilization of audio-visual materials, compulsory education on all levels, and the belief that schools should erect a positive system of rewards.

The Curriculum of the Schools in the City of the Sun

Unlike More and Rousseau, Campanella incorporated, in the *City of the Sun,* well-defined proposals regarding curriculum. However, Campanella felt as Plato did, that once a curriculum was erected it should not be changed. This is a recognizable weakness in the works of Campanella and Plato. However, it is understandable when one realizes that when these writers proposed their reform societies they felt that they had reached the ultimate in a human state.

All children from one to three years of age in the City of the Sun attended classes in which they were taught the alphabet. This teaching was aided by having the children walk around walls wherein the letters were inscribed.

The next period included children between the ages of three and seven years and consisted mainly of an extensive course in gymnastics to develop the body. The second course of study during this period consisted of an elaborate survey of all the trades and occupations within the state. The purpose of the occupational survey course was to determine the trend and interest of each student in regard to the choice of his future occupation. Campanella insisted upon the maxim that interest must be the first consideration in determining one's life work. However, he also felt that one's life-long occupation must be selected on the basis of one's abilities and talents. It is not an easy matter to determine the choice of a trade, and Campanella did not foresee or indicate any interest in a form of occupational testing. Therefore, it is understandable that he would devote four years of his curriculum to an occupational survey. The main criticism, however, rests upon Campanella's assumption that children between the age of three and seven could possibly indicate a mature judgment in regard to occupational choice.

The child at the age of seven entered a broad program of studies that ended only with the completion of those studies. This program of study was not divided into sections or schools such as elementary, junior high or senior high school. Campanella envisaged a developmental curriculum, which expanded the course content of the preceding school's course of studies.

The student began the program with an extensive study of mathematics. The study of mathematics continued throughout the entire program terminating when the student graduated. At the same time the student began to study mathematics he also began the study of science, a study which lasted throughout the entire educational program.

There is the suggestion in the *City of the Sun* that the students alternated their studies with courses in gymnastics and with community service. "While some are taking physical exercise," said Campanella, "or busying themselves with public services or functions, the others are engaged in attending the lectures."[31]

Campanella implied that there was a division between two areas. The first area corresponded to modern elementary and secondary school, and the second corresponded to a college program reminiscent of Plato's concept of advanced education wherein the advanced studies did not end with a four year program, but instead continued until the student could no longer profit from a higher education.

Essentially the curriculum, based upon the twelve divisions of knowledge,[32] was aimed at producing wise, free and civilized citizens. Campanella attempted to develop the course content in such a manner that liberty, knowledge, and culture would be the end result, but while this was his stated aim he did not relate how he would actualize it.

Campanella was too deeply engrossed in specific problems of education to see the broad value of foreign languages. Only a few scholars in the City of the Sun studied the various foreign languages. The majority of the students did not take languages as part of their course of studies.[33]

An important idea which contributed to the development of curriculum was Campanella's insistence upon the fact that students should cross departmental lines in their studies. In addition to science, which all students studied, everyone studied history, politics and philosophy.[34]

All students took courses in vocational education. Apprentice training was part of the occupational training. Students with a low intelligence received vocational training in one area, the area of farming. This was done mainly by means of apprentice training received on the farms. Campanella said, "Boys with retarded mentality are sent to the farms, and when they have improved, some are brought back to the city."[35]

Educational Opportunities for Women in the City of the Sun

The utopists have been united in their efforts to initiate equal political, social, and educational opportunities for women.

Campanella stated explicitly that women had equal opportunities at least in the area of education. The *City of the Sun* related, "Both sexes are educated together in all arts."[36]

Campanella felt that if women had equal rights in regard to education, it necessarily followed that women should attain equal opportunities in regard to occupations. Thus in the City of the Sun women held jobs on the basis of their ability rather than by virtue of their sex. However, Campanella limited the jobs that required great physical strength to men.[37] Individual differences were recognized in other occupations also. For example, needlework was performed exclusively by women.

An inconsistency in Campanella's thinking appeared when he stated that women should have equal educational opportunities, but he did not regard women as being equal socially. Primarily women had one role, to bear children. The function of child rearing was negated by Campanella for as soon as children were born they were removed to state nurseries. Women who could not have children were relegated to the lowest social class in the state.[38]

Freedom of choice in the area of marriage and family was denied to women. However, in the area of politics and education women were permitted virtually equal opportunities, but this is in keeping with Campanella's idea of having each person become as productive as possible in order to promote the welfare of the state, not because he was concerned with individual freedom.

Character Education in the City of the Sun

With the possible exception of vocational education there was not any area in the utopian educational schemes where there was more harmony of opinion than in the agreement of the need for courses in character education. Therefore, the utopists in general included in their writings well-developed techniques for character education.[39]

Fundamental to Campanella's philosophy of character education was the idea, initiated by Plato, that wrong acts were a direct resultant of a lack of knowledge. Campanella said, "People commit sins through lack of wisdom, or possibly by lack of love. Indeed, an individual sins out of ignorance."[40] It was imperative that people live good lives, for Campanella felt that wrong actions would ultimately destroy the state. "The sins of the people," said Campanella, "will redound to the disadvantage of the state."[41]

The basic contention of the utopists regarding character education was the agreement that it be positive. People must know the good, and further they must perform right actions not through fear, but through a desire to lead virtuous lives. Campanella stated emphatically that all moral acts must be performed through a right will. Fear per se was condemned in the City of the Sun. Fear was not used as a motivation to produce virtuous acts. Campanella stated, "The citizens of the City of the Sun have learned to put fear aside completely."[42]

The utopists in general related religious sanctions to character education. All of the proposed reform states contained detailed theological constructs. The medieval concept of the "great chain of being" which stemmed from Plato had a great effect upon Campanella. From the "chain of being" concept Campanella derived support for his authoritarian ethical system.

Campanella selected a limited list of virtues which he felt should be taught in the character education courses; he included magnanimity, fortitude, chastity,[43] wisdom,[44] charity, sobriety, and cheerfulness.[45] Throughout the city there were tablets dedicated to each of the virtues and inscribed with a definition of the virtue and means to encourage the development of good behavior.[46]

The curriculum of the schools included specific courses in character education.[47] Campanella stated that the courses in the main emphasized the philosophical basis for virtues and the theological basis for good and evil.[48] The text for the courses in moral development appeared to be St. Augustine's *City of God.* However, in general, Campanella felt that such injunctions as were used during his time were not only useless but detrimental to character development. The most detrimental injunction was the idea of hell which used fear as a vehicle. Students in the City of the Sun who misbehaved were corrected with love and tenderness.[49] Before any punishment could be meted out, however, the culprit was first made aware of his commission or omission. The technique was not merely punitive, but rather a form of educative process in moral development.

Vocational Education in the City of the Sun

Campanella was concerned with creating a reform state that would raise labor to a new dignity. Moreover, Campanella felt that it was the duty of the state of inaugurate economic policies that would make work easier and make each man more productive.

Campanella's attitude toward work prompted him to insist that all persons in his reform state should receive a vocational education that would make them productive and proud of their work.[50]

Several times in his book the *City of the Sun*, Campanella stated that a person who learned several trades received the highest honors the state could bestow. "A person who has learned several trades and knows how to practice them well is considered noble and outstanding."[51] Persons who became very adept in any occupation were made vocational teachers.[52]

Campanella held that society must have a high regard for all occupations. Tablets and pictures were displayed throughout the city lauding each and every occupation.[53] Extra praise was reserved for the more toilsome occupations, so that the students who chose onerous jobs were not relegated to a lower social class, thus farming was particularly held in high regard.[54]

Educational Psychology

The basic thesis of Campanella's psychology was the idea that love must be the cement of all social unions. He felt that motivation and discipline should not be based upon fear, but rather upon love. Children, who are motivated positively, that is, by love, are in a better position to achieve goals set for them. Love, gentleness and tenderness secure goals that fear cannot produce.[55]

The two major premises of Campanella's educational psychology regarding learning were: (1) learning would not take place by mere memorization, and (2) learning would not take place if books were the only source of material used. In speaking of the educational systems of his time Campanella leveled the following criticism:

> To gain knowledge in our time much servile labor and memory work is required, so that a man is rendered unskillful; since he has contemplated nothing but the works of books and has given his mind with useless result to the consideration of the dead signs of things.[56]

Campanella believed in utilizing nature. For example, children were sent out into the woods not only to play, but to see plants and trees actually growing. Books were important methods of instruction in More's scheme, but in the City of the Sun they were not the basic source. The world of nature was more important.

Campanella, along with all the utopists, believed that motivation must be positive. Learning had real significance when it solved practical situations. Students dealt with material from the real world which they actually experienced. They were compelled to see the educational data they were exposed to in terms of its ability to solve problems. Campanella felt that rewards in the form of recognition of success or rewards gained from social approbation was added impetus to learning.

Audio-Visual Materials and Methods

Campanella felt that education and teaching had to rely upon the senses. This being so, it is only natural that the use of visual materials be one of the main sources of education.

The first and primary visual tool was the one afforded by the walls which surrounded the city. The interior of the first wall was painted with mathematical figures. Alongside the figures an explanation was printed. The exterior side of the wall had a painting of the whole world. Along with this painting of the world there was a printed plaque for each country which included the country's history, its customs both private and public, its laws, and its language.

The second wall had pictures painted on its inside depicting precious and common stones, minerals, and metals. Wherever possible an actual specimen was included. On the outside of this wall there were pictures of all the seas, rivers, lakes, and streams of the world. Included with these were paintings of various fluids, as for example, oils. Printed alongside of the representation were the chemical constituents of the liquids. On top of one wall there were vials containing the fluids. The last of the pictorial representations on the second wall were of hail, snow, storms and thunder. Along with these productions there were stone representations of these phenomena.

The third wall had a picture and a specimen in a jar of every tree and herb grown in the world. Next to each specimen there was a tablet with the chemical constituents and the medicinal property of each. The exterior of the third wall had pictures and specimens of all the various fishes. The tablets alongside each listed their habits, commercial value, breeding habits and other pertinent information.

The fourth wall showed all the different kinds of birds and their habitat. The pictures were accurate in displaying them correctly as to size, color, nature, manner of living, etc. On the exterior of this wall there were pictures of all the insects in the world. The written explanations alongside the pictures included the habitat, uses, and poisonous qualities of each. Also this side of the wall had pictures of all types of reptiles.

The fifth wall had pictures of all remaining varieties of the animals found in the world. The animals were shown in their natural habitat.

The sixth wall showed all the mechanical arts. The tools used in each were also depicted. The use of the tools in different nations of the world was also shown. Along with each instrument or tool a statue of its inventor was displayed. Campanella elaborated in the following quotation:

> On the sixth interior are painted all the mechanical arts, with several instruments for each and their manner of use among different nations. Alongside the dignity of such is placed, and their several inventors are named, but on the exterior all the inventors in science, in warfare, and in law are represented.[57]

The education of the children was begun with their walking along the walls. All the citizens of the city also walk around in their leisure time. However, they walked about freely, whereas the children were led by a teacher who discussed the various representations. The use of charts, specimens, mock-ups, displays, and pictures to assist learning is basic to this educational system. All the citizens, regardless of age, were constantly motivated toward an understanding of the world, and of the useful arts by direct sense impression.

Among the more important educational ideas proposed by Campanella and which because of their practicality are part of modern educational practice the following are most significant.[58]

A system of educational psychology which emphasized sense

experience was proposed in the City of the Sun. The direct result of this position was to erect a school system wherein there was less reliance upon books as the primary source of information and more use of direct experience. Present-day schools follow this program of Campanella's by emphasizing, for example, the use of laboratories in science classes, field trips for social science classes, and other techniques that bring the student into direct contact with data. The use of various visual displays, including posters, drawings, zoos, museums, and botanical gardens was a natural outcome of Campanella's educational psychology. There has been a trend in modern school to utilize visual education.[59]

Campanella felt that vocational education was fundamental to the utopian idea that available resources, including men and materials, must be efficiently and completely utilized. Many modern schools include vocational education in the curriculum; the occupational courses operated on two levels: (1) training youth for future work, and (2) training those already employed who desire to raise their level of professional skills. Germany includes vocational education courses,[60] just as Italy, Australia, and the United States.[61]

Campanella believed that formal education should start early in a student's life. Thus, in the *City of the Sun* he proposed a program of pre-school training that suggested in many respects the modern kindergarten. He included in his program some training in the alphabet and numbers and a great deal of organized play which was intended to develop the body.

Campanella insisted that the curriculum of the elementary and secondary school include courses in physical education. Modern practices in the United States has tended to include more organized sports in physical education classes, whereas in Europe the movement has been closer to Campanella's idea of pure gymnastics. For example, certain European countries have extensive gymnastic programs in which all the youth participate: the Sokols in Czechoslovakia and the Falcons in Poland.

Academic recognition of the superior students was proposed in the *City of the Sun*. Contemporary honor lists and honor societies in secondary schools and colleges may be traced, in part, to suggestions such as Campanella's regarding the rewarding of high ability students.

Campanella was consistent with his stated aim that education was the most important activity for every person in his proposed state. He set up a school program that was compulsory and universal. Virtually every nation in the west and many countries such as India, Japan, and China, also have universal and compulsory school laws.[62] Equal educational opportunities for women was an integral part of Campanella's universal educational program, a factor also included in contemporary educational systems.[63]

The fundamental tenet of Campanella's philosophy was that every individual had the right to realize his potentialities. Campanella believed in equal opportunity and equal status for all the citizens of his new state. In order to give equal opportunities and to allow each person to develop his abilities he proposed a school program that included vocational education, the sciences and humanities. In effect, Campanella believed in a comprehensive school system; in part, the modern comprehensive secondary school has grown out of such suggestions contained in the *City of the Sun*.

Campanella proposed several ideas in the area of education that have not as yet been actualized, but which bear consideration for possible adoption.[64] Changing emphasis in education during the past two years is leaning in the direction Campanella proposed; for example, several of Campanella's suggestions are similar to those contained in the Conant Report.[65] Moreover, because of Campanella's belief in the efficacy of science as a means to exploit nature and assist in ordering the right type of society he required all the students in the City of the Sun to take courses in mathematics and science throughout their school life. However, Campanella naively did not see the problem of ability-grouping in these courses. Conant, in recommendation 19,[66] stated that all students should take courses in science and mathematics. (Conant, however, would have the students grouped by ability.)

Campanella proposed a program that in general was based upon a system of required classes for all, for example, vocational education, courses in language arts, etc. This proposal is similar to Conant's recommendation, 3,[67] wherein Dr. Conant proposed a system of required programs for all students.

In the City of the Sun all students were required to perform certain work for the good of the state. A period of public service performed by modern students bears study. To utilize this practice today the school would have to act as a coordinating agency resolving legal, social, health, and moral aspects related to public service and place students in activities that would meet the need of the community as well as provide a learning situation for each student.

Campanella was concerned with the fact that there should be no gap between the academic disciplines.[68] Campanella realized that interest would lead certain students to specialize, but he wanted each student to have an understanding of the humanities as well as the sciences regardless of their major area of concern. In the past European schools had a tendency to lessen the gap between the disciplines,[69] while education in America, particularly higher education, tended to produce specialists.[70] However, in the last several years there has been a movement toward the aim proposed by Campanella. There is a trend toward narrowing the gap between the disciplines. Many colleges are now requiring, in the form of basic courses, a period of studies in the foundations of the sciences, social sciences, and liberal arts.

The last proposal made by Campanella (and after careful study might be included in contemporary pedagogical practices), was the idea that superior students receive social recognition. Campanella believed that high ability students who performed at the peak of their abilities should receive recognition not just within the school, but throughout the state. Awards, within the students' community, might be set up, for example, in the form of banquets, or other honors. Recognition of superior attainment might be made a permanent part of the student's diploma as suggested by Dr. Conant.[71] As Dr. Conant pointed out this recognition should also include those who have indicated superior attainment in the vocational and commercial arts field.[72]

Summary and Conclusions

Utopian proposals share, along with any new idea, a requirement to be critically examined in regard to their value not in terms of their novelty, but in terms of their power to contribute materially to social betterment. There was much that was impossible in Campanella's scheme; nevertheless, the theme that is recurrent in the *City of the Sun* is that men can by themselves prevent social disaster. Campanella proposed much that was of value, for example, the idea of legal and constitutional rights, the advocacy of the fullest possible utilization of both human and natural resources, and the stress upon the application of science to society. Campanella believed that men could control not only the natural environment, but could of their own free will change their society, by learning and controlling the laws of human nature. Campanella felt that most of the laws of human behavior were subject to verification in the same manner as were, for instance, the laws of physics. The agencies of the City were based upon psychological laws. This chapter contains, in the way of illustration, a detailed analysis of scientific and psychological laws applied by Campanella to the family and marriage. Rather than relegate reproduction to a capricious social pattern of behavior Campanella was the first to propose scientific principles of eugenics. He was the prophet of the modern eugenic movement.

Laidler stated that among the most important ideas of the *City of the Sun* is the idea that:

> The government is in the hands of the aristocracy of learning, elected by the people, and the chief of the temporal and spiritual affairs of the state must be informed concerning practically every branch of knowledge known to that day.[73]

The factor of sociability in the City of the Sun reaches the high state that Plato proposed for his guardians and magistrates, and by virtually the same means, and that is a benevolent brotherhood based upon commonality of property and elimination of family life. Campanella failed to recognize the importance of family and social life; his advocacy of holding women in common and the destruction of marriage is impossible if for no other reason than it is in direct opposition to the social custom of monogamy,[74] and for the subsequent parental feelings engendered by the birth of children. Equally naive was Campanella's suggestion that citizens could exist in a society that made privacy virtually illegal. Dormitory and barrack life is useful in situations of emergency, but the need for privacy and seclusion appear to be deep-seated in human nature and provisions for them must be made in any efficient society. Campanella could only perceive of people in terms of groups, never as individuals. He denied the right to individuality and made each person a cog in the machine, a cog that was expendable. He advocated compulsory participation in every social activity, even education. For example, it appeared that every adult was required to attend daily lectures. No provision was made to arouse interest. Everybody attended the same lecture at the same time. As a whole Campanella proposed a primitivistic, agrarian and thoroughly communistic society relieved only by possessing Christian theology and ethics. However, if for nothing else we owe to Campanella the idea that anything, including the perfectability of human nature and the state, was possible if men would only will it.

chapter five

THE NATURE OF THE CONCEPT IN THE *CHRISTIANOPOLIS*

PUBLISHED IN 1618, the *Christianopolis* is the work of a man who was able to put into practice in his own lifetime many of the ideas contained in his utopia. It has been said of Andreae that he was:

> One of the first to divine the dawn of a new epoch in the history of human civilization and to give expression to the secret hopes and aspirations of his time by the creation of a utopia.[1]

The seventeenth century has been called by Whitehead the century of genius.[2] What is the nature of the man who could, in this period of intellectual greatness, analyze the needs of his time and propose one of the few truly original utopias ever written?

Andreae was born on August 17, 1586. He attended the university at Tübingen where he specialized in languages, history, and mathematics. Andreae was well versed in Latin, Greek, Hebrew, French, Spanish, Italian, and English. Mathematics held a great deal of interest for Andreae. Prior to the publication of his utopia Andreae published a series of lectures dealing with mathematics, the *Collectanea Mathematica*.[3] Andreae also corresponded with Kepler throughout the latter's life. Mathematics held an important position in Andreae's educational reforms, as they did in Plato's *Republic*. Andreae traveled for several years after leaving the university. He visited Switzerland, among other places, where he was impressed with the social conditions of the country. Andreae went to Calw in 1620 as a minister of a Lutheran church. He attempted to put into practice many of his ideas and in particular those related to social and educational reform. For example, he founded a mutual protective association among the workers in the factories in Calw. This association functioned into the nineteenth century. Andreae died in 1650.

Andreae's Plan for the Improvement of the Human Community

Christianopolis began with an analysis of the world situation. Andreae was distressed with the condition of man. He felt that the church, the government, the people, and even the universities of his time, were characterized by unscrupulous ambition, greed, gluttony, license, and ". . . other mastering vices at which Christ violently shuddered, but in which men delighted."[4] The fault that was most reprehensible was pride, for Andreae considered it the forerunner of a closed mind.

Andreae proposed a new society, a society that would elevate man to the level that Andreae felt God intended for man. Andreae intended for Christianopolis to be a theocratic utopian state. The dominant theme of Andreae's book is that Christianopolis was the realization of the City of God on earth. The citizens of this utopian community would have to have the highest moral character. They would have to possess a great deal of knowledge, and lastly they would have to be able to operate in a free manner within the limits of moral, natural, and community law. Andreae proposed that the "right" type of education could produce the desired type of citizens. It is the purpose of this chapter to examine what Andreae meant by the "right" type of education. However, since schools do not operate in a vacuum, it is important to note the social conditions Andreae proposed to intiate.

Plato and Campanella eliminated the idea of family life from their utopias, but contrariwise Andreae believed that the family was the foundation of the state.[5] The foundation of family life resided in the piety of the partners. The demand for piety was also the basis for mate selection. In a sense, piety was the dowery the spouse brought into the marriage, for moral goodness was one of the most prized possessions in the state. The primary function of marriage was to produce children.[6] Andreae took Christ's injunction against adultery literally and stated that adultery could take place even in a marriage where the partners allowed passion to motivate their behavior. A person could make a sin out of lawful practices[7] by distorting them. Thus, sex in marriage was to be used for reproduction and not for an end in itself. Mutual love tempered with Christian piety was to be the rule within the family of Christianopolis.

Because women tend to outlive their husbands, Andreae included courses in the area of vocational education for widows. Andreae was the first of the utopists to be concerned with widowhood and with the aged in general. The aged were given honor and respect in the proposed new state. They received special foods, housing and care. Special seats were reserved for the aged at the banquets, entertainments and other festivals. Young people were taught to show respect and special consideration for the elderly.

Andreae was the first utopist to describe and propose facilities for the care of the sick. The *Christianopolis* contained an original medical concept. It was the idea of a hygienic, aseptic hospital.[8] The hospital staff included dietitians, surgeons, and physicians. Operations were performed under the most sterile conditions. Special workers trained in psychology and theology were assigned to the hospital; their job was to work with the patients and to attempt to cheer them, to help them see that sickness was part of the divine plan, and to accept it philosophically.[9]

Everything that took place in Christianopolis was seen in theological context. The religion of the citizens of Andreae's new state was Protestant and closely allied to the Lutheran Church.[10] The citizens assembled three times a day—morning, noon, and night—for devotional prayers and Scriptural readings. All the people regardless of age had to attend the prayer meetings which lasted for a half-hour.[11] Andreae stated that while private prayers were acceptable, the best form of prayer and the type preferred by God was public prayer. Throughout the city there were tablets imprinted with the creed and theology of the state religion.[12] The citizens were constantly reminded of their duties in regard to Christian charity and Christian fellowship.

Not only was Christian charity evidenced in the treatment of the sick, but also in the care of the aged, and in the economic pattern of the state.

Basically Christianopolis had an agrarian economy. Agriculture fitted into the utopian scheme of things because it represented the closest tie any man could have with nature. Agriculture for Andreae was also a truly egalitarian occupation. Christianopolis utilized a communal basis for the distribution of goods. No form of money or monetary exchange was used. Goods were stored in central storage facilities. Distribution was based upon need. Unlike the inhabitants of the City of the Sun the citizens of Christianopolis had a great deal of privacy. They lived in private homes and ate their meals in their own homes, but they drew their provisions from the public storehouses.[13] The homes were not owned by the inhabitants and from time to time the state required that people change residences so that they would not form too deep an association with material things.

The government of Christianopolis was based on a form of representative democracy. The constitution was based upon three fundamental precepts: ". . . equality, the desire for peace, and the contempt for riches."[14]

The governmental leaders were chosen by the citizens. Those elected to office had to be of the highest caliber. The leaders were reminiscent of Plato's philosopher-king in that the members of Christianopolis expected its chief and senate to be the intellectual elite of the state.

The state was ruled by a triumvirate elected in a general election.[15] Andreae said:

> The triumvirate is the safest form of government when it admits only the best in the state and those experienced in public affairs, since one must work up through all steps of virtue to it.[16]

The three men were responsible for the various divisions of the state. The first was concerned with education, the second with religion, and the third with justice. Each man had a group of advisors to assist him in making decisions and carrying them out. The leaders who were selected had to have the highest character and intellectual qualities for they were enjoined to ". . . propagate the Gospel, to protect their subjects, to ennoble the youth, adorn the land, and to increase the number of dwellers in heaven."[17]

The purpose of the state was to supply the spiritual, economic, social and cultural fulfillment for the citizens. Andreae felt that education would produce a cultured, moral citizenry who would live in peace, follow virtuous lives and reproduce moral, intelligent, healthy children. Andreae charged education with a heavy burden. The remainder of this chapter will examine the educational system of the proposed reform state, in order to indicate how education would produce the desired type of citizens, and to what extent the ideas have been actualized.

Educational Philosophy in the Christianopolis

The basic theme of the Christianopolis was that a superior system of education will tend to produce superior citizens.[18] The role of the schools was to foster moral development, encourage the pursuit of the humanities, teach an occupation, and develop and expand the sciences.

Andreae stated that education was the central activity of the state.[19] The physical center of the proposed state was occupied by a large building. The streets of the city led to the center, since the city was designed to form a wheel; the hub comprised the largest building in the metropolis and the streets formed the spokes.[20] The hub contained the college, the secondary and primary school as well as the administration offices, the laboratories and other related offices.[21]

Andreae, standing as he did in the new epoch, attempted to formulate an educational philosophy that utilized the scientific method as a touchstone. Andreae was the first of the seventeenth-century writers to apply the scientific method to evaluate and to propose new educational methods and content, as well as to apply the method to develop a new theology, a system of government and a new, social and economic life.

Fundamentally Andreae's creed was stated in the *Christianopolis* thus:

> Unless you analyze matter by experiment, unless you improve the deficiencies of knowledge by more capable instruments you are worthless.[22]

Andreae made science a tool and a criterion for the expansion of knowledge, just as Bacon did. Andreae said, "You must test nature, everything that the earth contains is subjected to the laws and instruments of science."[23] A questioning mind for Andreae was the end result of education.[24] Christianopolis was a utopia that was not static; it grew, and science helped to point the way to live in a changing world. Science possessed the tools to exploit nature. Science, for Andreae, was the means to discover a new philosophy containing a rational theology that would create sound principles to regulate and order society; for ultimately Andreae desired to create a scientific theocracy. Science was for Andreae the criterion for erecting his curriculum, and it was the main constituent of the curriculum.

Andreae felt that the aim of the perfect state, of the perfect educational system, and of God's purpose for man, could only be realized if man examined the underlying principles of the good in terms of scientific principles.

The School System in the Christianopolis

The educational system was under the direct supervision of a member of the triumvirate. Thus, the director of learning included in his duties the control of the school system as well as a major share of the governing of the state.[25] The director of learning had several assistants.[26] The assistants were responsible for their own departments.

The first department was responsible for the curriculum. The curriculum department had twelve sub-departments. They were mathematics, biological science, natural science, philosophy, ethics and theology, music, grammar, history, political science, languages, and the professional schools which included medicine, law and nursing.

The remaining departments included vocational education,

audio-visual materials, character education, laboratories, libraries, museums, and botanical gardens.[27]

The school system was divided into four sections: pre-school, elementary school, secondary school, and the university. Children began their education at the age of six.[28] At this age they were taken from their parents and placed under the supervision of teachers who also were in charge of the dormitories. The young boys were placed under the direction of married men teachers, whose wives were also teachers who directed the young girls. The students lived in small groups with the teacher directing all their activities, social as well as educational.

The secondary school was located in the central college building. However, there were vocational education shops, science laboratories, and other specialized school buildings throughout the city that were used in conjunction with the secondary curriculum.

Andreae stated explicitly that the school plant should be clean, large, and attractive.[29] He was concerned about the fact that it appeared to be a natural law that people desired to raise their children under the best possible conditions; they endeavored to give their children the best foods, plenty of rest, etc. Why then, were people content with inferior forms of education? Andreae's utopia was different, for it:

> considered the most important of all duties to be education, thus they have furnished elaborate schools that they might declare their love and care for these, their children.[30]

Andreae felt that the people of his time while insisting that they loved their children, shut them up in schools that were ". . . unhealthy, and even a dirty prison."[31] The schools of Christianopolis were ". . . open, sunny, and happy, so that with the sight of pictures, even, they attract the children, fashion the minds of boys and girls, and advise the youths."[32]

Andreae held that the development of the finest schools, teachers, and equipment available was an investment that would be realized when the children took their place in society as moral, cultured and productive citizens.

The teachers of Christianopolis were selected by the citizens on the basis of rigid qualifications. The qualifications included scholastic ability, dignity, integrity, enthusiasm, energy, and kindness.[33] Andreae elaborated upon the personal qualities of the teachers in the following quotation:

> The teachers must excel others in reverence toward God, uprightness toward their neighbor, in moderation and virtue, in skill and wisdom, and must have the highest power of judgment for instruction and education, as well as a recognition of the personality and problems of their pupils. They must prefer to spur their charges on as free agents, with kindness, courteous treatment, and a liberal discipline rather than with threats, blows, and like sternness.[34]

The school day began with a prayer. The day was then divided for each student so that it included classroom work, study periods (held in the morning for boys and in the afternoon for girls), vocational education courses, and gymnastic classes and exercises.[35]

The Curriculum of the Schools in the Christianopolis

The most significant contribution to the history of educational ideas and reform made by Andreae was in the area of curriculum development. The curriculum is the basis of the school, and it would appear obvious that the analytical character of Andreae's mind would naturally lead him to question and develop the essentials in education. Fundamentally, Andreae was a practical man; as indicated earlier, he put his ideas into practice as in the case of the worker's cooperative and the elementary school which he founded. The curriculum proposed in the *Christianopolis* reflected Andreae's practical nature, for it is essentially dedicated to problem-solving. Essentially the curriculum espoused the scientific method. Even the subject of theology was subjected to scientific verification, or at least Andreae felt he subjected it to the method of scientific inquiry. He stated:

> What a narrow thing is human knowledge if it walks about as a stranger in the most wholesome creations and does not know what advantage this or that thing bears to man, yet

meanwhile wanders about in the unpleasant crackle of abstractions and rules, none the less boasting of this as a science of the highest order! It should rather be the aim, after something has been accomplished with that theory, to prove its practical value to men.[36]

In the elementary school the curriculum was composed of courses in the following subjects: character education, grammar, mathematics, music, history, science, and gymnastics.[37]

The secondary school curriculum was the same as the elementary school curriculum with the addition of biology, chemistry, physics, languages, and advanced courses in mathematics, for example, geometry.[38]

Andreae discussed the curriculum of the university in great detail. The most original contribution was the inclusion of courses in political science in the curriculum and the idea of a professional college including a medical school and a school of nursing.

1. The curriculum in the secondary schools.

The first course which Andreae included in the curriculum was grammar. Grammar was taught at all levels, but in the secondary schools Latin, Greek, and Hebrew were taught in conjunction with it. Andreae specifically stated that these three languages were to be taught as part of the work in grammar,[39] because he felt these languages were practical in that they helped to train the mind in formulating thought.[40] For example, he felt that Latin possessed the ability to make the mind incisive because of its grammatical rules and usage.[41]

Students in the secondary schools were taught courses in speech, for Andreae felt that ". . . speech is an indication of thought."[42] Andreae believed that by improving one's ability to speak the thought processes would likewise be improved. Andreae stated that the basic rule for oratory was that all speeches and conversations should be simple and direct.[43]

The secondary school curriculum included a course in logic. This was, in the main, a study of the scientific method. Andreae's views regarding this course are expressed in the following passage:

> The students learn to apply the scientific method to every variety of human affairs, to classify whatever is given them, then to form syllogisms that they may see what is necessarily true, what is possible, and where some fallacy of judgment lurks.[44]

Andreae's description of the course of logic leads one to assume that he felt that if the student, and ultimately the citizen, knows the method of attaining the truth (that is, the scientific method), he need have no higher authority to appeal to than his own reason. The citizens of utopia were free because they have knowledge of the truth. They knew truth because they have the means to test it. Andreae said, "Let us in truth love the truth, for man has within him the great treasure of judging truth."[45] Andreae represents the intellectual tradition of the seventeenth century which was in revolt against the type of authority displayed by the Church and by existing monarchies. In effect, Andreae wanted to erect an authority of reason which when aided by scientific method could arbitrate all intellectual, moral, religious and ethical disputes.

Mathematics was a necessary course because as Andreae said, "If you consider human need there is no branch of knowledge to which mathematics does not bear some importance."[46] For example, Andreae felt that geometry was important in theoretical research and as an aid in the solution of practical problems.[47]

The study of arithmetic and geometry was a prerequisite to the study of music. Andreae included the study of religious poetry in the course of music. The students were taught to sing in chorus because the choral groups were part of the daily prayer meetings.[48]

Physics included astronomy and was taught in the last year of the secondary school. Related to physics were courses grouped under what Andreae called natural science. These courses included geology, with emphasis on minerology[49] and courses related to the building and construction trades.

Biology and chemistry were important in the curriculum because they gave man the tools to exploit nature, and formed the basis for the study of genetics, disease, and sanitation, factors which Andreae considered important in creating the perfect state.[50]

The final course in the secondary school was history. Andreae felt that no other subject was more distorted than history. Historians had changed history so that countries would appear in the best light, but in Christianopolis history was taught objectively: ". . . everything was written down very plainly, and the citizens confess all their doings, even their faults, frankly in order than posterity may know the events of the past without disguise."[51] History was taught in order that principles could be derived from the lessons of the past that would be applicable in solving current problems.[52]

2. The curriculum in the university.

The courses included in the secondary curriculum were also part of the university curriculum. However, these courses were offered on an advanced level. Andreae stated without giving reasons that the high school and college program offered no electives.

Language courses in Christianopolis were taken by all students. The foreign language department included both modern and classical languages. Andreae envisaged a reform state that was not as isolated from the world as was the *City of the Sun*. Thus, modern languages were of assistance in commerce and in exchanging ideas with foreign countries.

Philosophy was required of all students because of its ontological significance and as an adjunct to science and social life. Andreae divided philosophy into ethics, metaphysics, theology, and logic.

Students studied Christian ethics because Andreae felt that it was to be their ". . . guide in all human virtues, in prudence, justice, moderation, bravery, and kindred qualities."[53] Basically the study of ethics was to give to each person the proper attitude and the proper means to live a well-regulated life, for ultimately happiness was individualistic, and if the citizens collectively were unhappy the state would suffer. Andreae tells us:

> This is true, no one else is to blame for our unhappiness except ourselves, we must pray God that we may live a moral and well-regulated life.[54]

Metaphysics was the study of the ". . . true, the good, the beautiful, unity and order."[55] Andreae included the study of first causes—cosmology and aesthetics—in the course of metaphysics.

Logic was primarily the study and application of the scientific method.

Theology, referred to by Andreae as ". . . the queen of all that human beings possess, and the mistress of philosophy,"[56] was a required subject for all university students. It was inevitable that Andreae would make theology a required course for the development of the various proposals incorporated in the *Christianopolis* based upon supernatural foundation and purpose. The entelechy of Christianopolis was Christianity. The theological course was divided into three areas.[57] The first area was biblical interpretation and typology. The students studied the literal meaning of the Bible, but they also studied the Bible from a tropological, allegorical, and anagogical point of view. The second general area covered in the course was meditation. The last area was apologetics. This appears to be the most important field. While the state of Christianopolis permitted religious freedom Andreae was anxious about heresy. The students were taught the foundations of their religion and were expected to defend it. Andreae never named his branch of Christianity. He revealed:

> The citizens of Christianopolis avoid names of sects especially, nor do they at all willingly pronounce them; and though they love to hear the name of Lutheran, yet they strive first of all to be Christians.[58]

Political science,[59] including political history, theory, and government was a major contribution which Andreae among others made to curriculum development. Andreae proposed the revolutionary idea that men could learn the techniques by which to govern other men. It is important to note that the times in which Andreae lived were suffused with the idea of the divine right of kings. If the *Christianopolis* contained no other idea than that of the scientific study of government, it would still justify its inclusion in the list of classic utopias.[60]

The last major idea developed by Andreae in this area was the idea of a professional school attached to the university. The college in Christianopolis contained the schools of medicine, nursing, law, and pharmacy.

The school of medicine also included a well-developed section of surgery. Andreae had many original ideas related to medicine, including the idea of hygiene and asepsis, diet as a cure for many illnesses. Psychosomatic medicine, as well as the idea that surgery was a vital adjunct to medicine, were other proposals made by Andreae.

A school of pharmacy was included in the graduate school and operated in conjunction with the school of medicine.[61] A school of nursing was part of the over-all health program of Christianopolis. In the main, the school of nursing graduated female nurses, but it appeared that men were also trained.[62]

A school of law was proposed by Andreae. He stated that students trained in law entered the governmental service, for there was little need for tort, contract, or criminal litigation in Christianopolis. Andreae felt that the school of law should be a graduate school of political science and he stated that the students should study political history and rules of government, rather than study legal precedent or a *corpus juris*.[63]

Andreae proposed a curriculum that supposed each course was important and therefore he eliminated electives from his school system. The curriculum contained courses in the sciences and in the humanities, for Andreae decided that his school would produce well-rounded citizens. He said:

> The citizens of Christianopolis want firmly-rooted natures and they obtain these through a liberal education; in this way the memory is strengthened, power of judgment is strengthened, power of judgment is drawn forth, individual frankness is fostered, and work is gradually adapted to the talents.[64]

Andreae was aware of the fact that a curriculum that did not provide an elective system would have difficulty in meeting the needs of the students because of their different abilities, interests and levels of attainment. His solution was to devise a curriculum that contained every provision for every contingency. He was unable to perceive the time when any individual would, because of the accumulation of knowledge, be unable to absorb it all. He naively stated that the citizens of Christianopolis should:

> provide themselves with all the liberal arts, and they love to arrange them rationally and in orderly manner, and when there is need when a problem arises, draw them forth one at a time from their several places and use them to solve the need.[65]

Throughout Andreae's discussion of this proposed curriculum he made the purpose of the courses teleological in very explicit terms. The solution of problems, the ability to live harmoniously in the new polis, were secondary benefits derived from the course of studies. The glorification of God and the salvation of the soul was the primary goal.

Educational Opportunities for Women in Christianopolis

Andreae stated that women would have equal education, as well as occupational, social and political opportunities in his new state. Andreae's particular contribution was not only to offer equality of opportunity for women, but he went even further and insisted that the state be more solicitous of their welfare, especially in the areas in which they were most exposed to the whims of chance, namely, pregnancy, childbirth, widowhood, and old age. The curriculum included courses to help women in these areas.

Education was compulsory in Christianopolis for both sexes. Women attended the secondary school, and those who possessed ability entered the college.[66] Andreae stated that women should be given the opportunity of becoming teachers. However, Andreae made it plain that the ultimate end of women was to become mothers and wives. The idea is rampant in the *Christianopolis* that education, both in the humanities and sciences, would endow the citizens with the intellectual tools needed to adjust to life, to entertain one's self as well as to entertain others, and in addition to entertain new ideas. It is thus axiomatic that women must have the greatest amount of education they were capable of receiving if they were to fulfill adequately their role in the family as well as be able to enjoy and share equally full political and economic status.

It is possible to discover the attributes Andreae desired in women by analyzing the character of the two women he set up as models. The first woman Andreae chose to have the female citizens of Christianopolis emulate was Mary, the mother of Christ. Mary possessed the attributes of a peaceful nature, a loving disposition, and a proper attitude during her widowhood, along with many other fine qualities. The second woman that Andreae used as a model was Monica, the mother of St. Augustine. Her qualities included dedication to the church, generosity toward her children, peace with her husband, charity and loyalty, intelligence and wisdom; and, as in the case of Mary, she possessed the proper attitude toward her widowhood. The foregoing list of virtues did not imply that Andreae desired women to be docile or meek. Rather, he preferred a strong sense of Christian humility.

Andreae argued forcibly that women in the state of widowhood must be given assistance.

In the main, the schools had the duty to equip women with the skills needed in the last phase of their life. While it would appear from a cursory examination of the discussion of widowhood in the *Christianopolis* that widow's skills were needed in such positions as dormitory supervisors, a more thorough investigation indicated that the real reason for the employment of these women was psychological. Andreae felt that employment was the best means to overcome grief.

Andreae was imbued with the philosophy of Plato, and the idea of justice and harmony which was rampant in the *Republic*, was, in turn, responsible for the concept of balance in the *Christianopolis*. Every citizen had a responsibility to the whole. The polis was the life of the citizens; even community prayer was considered more efficacious than solitary prayer. Thus, a woman (or man) was expected to continue to be active, to perform her role, in order that the whole might continue.[67] Paramount in utopian psychology was the idea that each person must seek his own happiness, for an unhappy person can neither be good nor effective. The utopian law proposed, "One must be happy first, then one can be good." Thus, widows who were busy and who felt they were needed and wanted had a chance to be happy.

Widows had the opportunity to attend school[68] and to study nursing, midwifery, or other skills such as sewing, cooking, and diet management. They could work in the nurseries or in the dormitories. These women could also attend the university preparatory to becoming teachers.

Certain sections of the *Christianopolis* seem to be a handbook on some aspects of nursing, for Andreae gave a complete description of the needs and care of pregnant women. He believed, "The crowning accomplishment of women was bearing of children."[69] He was inconsistent in his attitude toward women, for ultimately he preferred women to be docile, clean, healthy wives capable of bearing many healthy children rather than intellectually equal members of the state.

Character Education in the Christianopolis.

Is it possible for a state that ignores the moral training of its citizens to survive? To this question each of the utopists emphatically answered, "No!" Andreae considered character education as one of the most important courses in his proposed curriculum. He referred to it as practical theology.[70]

A course in moral and character education was included in the studies in the elementary school, secondary school, as well as in the college. The course was divided into the areas of exegesis, eschatology, and rules of conduct.

The major part of the time spent in the course was devoted to defining the good, for Andreae was imbued with the Platonic idea that knowledge of the good would tend to produce right performances. The greatest good possessed by any citizen was virtue.[71] The elite arrived at their station in Christianopolis not through the accumulation of material goods, but by assiduous cultivation of virtue. As has already been indicated the dowry brought to the marriage was piety. Following the Greek tradition Andreae defined moderation as the chief virtue.[72] The remaining virtues which were taught in the schools included patience, devotion, loyalty, knowledge, chastity, truth, honor, and fraternity. The list of virtues seems to agree with those virtues held by Christian tradition. However, Andreae emphasized fraternity[73] and this was probably due to the fact that his new state was based upon the concept of inter-personal contact.

Two powerful influences on good behavior were the respect for and the status achieved by virtuous conduct.[74] Citizens who excelled in good conduct were held in esteem as models from which the students could pattern their own lives. The general moral tone of the populace, Andreae naively assumed, would cause the young people to emulate the behavioral patterns prescribed for them.[75] Throughout the city tablets, which were imprinted with moral rules, were attached to buildings, posts, etc.[76]

There was no system of punishment incorporated in the judicial system of the proposed state. Andreae felt that punishment was usually meted out in society not to correct the wrongdoer, but to revenge the wronged party.[77] He stated that if punishments were to be set up they should be relative to the individual, for to erect a standard form of punishment ignored the very important psychological framework on which Christianopolis operated, namely, that each person was different. It was felt that punishment should fit the individual and not the offense. Another thing that bothered Andreae was the fact that his contemporary society classified the destruction of property as the most heinous crime of all, whereas offenses against the person, including murder and rape, were considered as less important.[78] Andreae was horrified that property was treated as more important than people. The wrongdoer in Christianopolis was made to see, by means of reason, the errors that had been committed and to desire to correct his behavior. The worst possible punishment was excommunication and banishment.[79]

Ultimately Andreae believed that the success of character education rested upon each person being educated to the point where he would take pride in controlling concupiscence.[80] Each student was taught that in cultivating a dignified, cultured nature, in dominating desire, he would be able to participate with greater joy in the fellowship of the polis. Andreae insisted that a "refined soul" would feel "unspeakable joy" in renouncing worldly pleasure.[81] Andreae failed to see that his idea was impossible, for this pattern of behavior is possible of achievement only by a handful of mystics and not by a large state.

Fundamentally the students were taught that the transitory pleasure of acquiescing to concupiscence was negligible to the long-term joy of cultivating a virtuous nature.

Vocational Education in the Christianopolis

A fundamental tenet in the utopian philosophy is the dignity of labor; consequently, each classic utopian scheme included a system of vocational education.

The philosophical basis, upon which the courses of vocational education were devised, held that work was not merely a means of production, it was a way in which men and women could express their creative, inventive, and artistic abilities. Andreae said:

> Work is done not always because necessity demands it, but in order that the human soul may have some means by which it and the highest prerogative of the mind may unfold itself through different sorts of machinery, or by which the little spark of divinity remaining in us, may whine brightly in any material offered.[82]

Several utopists dignified labor by instituting one basic form of employment for all citizens, usually agricultural work. Andreae differed from the utopian tradition in that he utilized the technique of involving the whole polis in work. He said:

> The whole city is, as it were, one single workshop, but of all different sorts of crafts. If the supply of material is sufficient the workmen are permitted to indulge and give play to their inventive genius.[83]

The elementary school program included manual arts for boys and domestic arts for the girls.[84] It wasn't until secondary school that students could take courses in the vocational area of their choice. Each student, male and female, took a series of courses to prepare him for a job since each person in Christianopolis had to work.[85]

Before a student chose the occupational area in which he majored, he went through a period of counseling and guidance. During the period of vocational guidance the student was made to realize that his occupation was not a mere livelihood for himself, but it was an important function for the whole community and a way of glorifying God.[86]

Added to the particular work of each person were duties which were relative to the over-all functioning of the state and in which every citizen engaged. For example:

> "There are also public duties," said Andreae, "to which all citizens have obligation, such as guarding, harvesting of grain, working roads, erecting public buildings, draining ground, etc., which are imposed on all in turn according to age and sex, but not very often nor for a long time."[87]

Thus, in a sense, public work, which included agricultural employment, was used by Andreae—as it was by More and Campanella—to elevate the dignity of labor and to eliminate class and status symbols based upon employment.

Andreae stated explicitly that the same amount of intelligence was required for the occupation of mechanic, for example, as was needed for employment in the sciences.[88] However, he felt that some men for various reasons became specialists in their jobs, and these men in Christianopolis were the teachers of their specialties.[89]

Women worked also, but in the main their courses were related to the domestic area, and jobs such as those that entailed sewing or cooking were reserved exclusively for them.[90]

Andreae wrote in his Christianopolis that education had to prepare men to live effectively in their chosen society. In order to educate the whole man, the schools had to impart to him the techniques which would enable him to live a cultured, moral and useful life. Vocational education was included in the curriculum because Andreae felt that it gave men the training needed in becoming useful, and it also supplied the materials for creative expression.

Audio-Visual Materials and Methods in the Christianopolis

Andreae included a system of visual methods and materials in his educational system. He did not believe, for example, that a museum should exist as a separate building, apart from the daily life of the people. He wanted the whole city itself to be a museum which would include art treasures, educational displays, etc.

There were tablets displayed throughout the city which bore the inscriptions of moral precepts, laws, and commentaries of significant scientific, historical, or educational interest.

It would have been impractical to display some things in the open area of the city. Therefore, Andreae proposed several buildings which corresponded to our modern concept of the museum,[91] in that many historical remains, fossils, relics, etc., were preserved there. However, these buildings were also libraries. Located near the libraries were the buildings which housed the printing and binding shops.[92]

Laboratories were an important adjunct to the school of science. Chemistry workrooms were housed in a special building. The laboratories included facilities for analyzing the properties of metals, minerals and vegetables.[93] Another building held the laboratories which were devoted to the study of biology. Connected with this laboratory was the anatomy area which was used by the medical school.[94] The study of mathematics also had its own laboratory which contained rooms devoted to the study of astronomy. A planetarium was also included,[95] and a special laboratory was reserved for physics.[96]

The city was laid out in such a manner that botanical gardens and zoological parks were dispersed throughout the area. The citizens wandered throughout the gardens and zoological parks, leisurely investigating the specimens found there.

The *Christianopolis* contained several worthy educational ideas that have been accepted in modern pedagogic practices. The first educational proposal was concerned with the school plant. Andreae stated that the school must first of all conform to certain aesthetic and hygienic standards. Included in the health standards were requirements related to the cleanliness, amount of light and air admitted, size, and location. The aesthetic requirements included the very important idea that the school must be attractive. The building itself, as well as the surrounding grounds, enhanced the general learning atmosphere. Pleasant surroundings promote the desire to learn.[97]

Andreae insisted that teachers must be well trained.[98] The critical shortage of teachers after World War II tended to slow down the movement toward higher academic and personality requirements for teachers. However, there has been a general trend toward the realization of Andreae's goal, particularly in the past one hundred years. Teacher training in the United States, Canada, Europe and Russia has been approaching the stage where teachers must possess a bachelor's degree or its equivalent.

Andreae introduced two new courses in the *Christianopolis*: (1) a course in speech, and (2) a course in political science. While these courses are a part of most modern colleges and secondary school curriculum, their novelty is overshadowed by Andreae's most important educational idea. The *Christianopolis* contained, in basic form, the plans for the modern university, composed of several colleges. Among the colleges Andreae suggested were those of medicine, pharmacy, and nursing. This was a completely new idea, but it required several centuries before it was actualized.[99]

Andreae, standing at the dawn of a modern science, and perceiving the dangers of a society or educational program too deeply committed only to one branch of knowledge, proposed that the schools balance the scientific studies with the humanities. The history of western education from Andreae's time to the present has followed his precept; modern educational ideals still attempt to educate the whole man by balancing the humanities with the sciences.

In the main, the major educational ideas contained in the *Christianopolis* that have value, but which are yet actualized,[100] include the inclusion in the curriculum of a course in logic as well as a required course in the scientific method offered at all school levels. Andreae wanted to teach his students how to think; therefore, he insisted that the courses in logic and scientific method be taught in the elementary and secondary schools as well as in the colleges. Related to these courses was a class in ethics. Andreae not only wanted men to know how to think, but he wanted them to think well. Another course that Andreae felt should be required for all students was speech. Andreae perceived a relationship between thinking well and speaking well. The problem of speech has to a great extent been neglected in the area of communication. Wendell Johnson,[101] in the area of semantics, attributed virtually all neurosis to the problem of inadequate speech. If the schools are to be concerned with the problem of mental health there must be more concern over the inclusion of required courses in the area of speech.

Summary and Conclusions

Andreae realized the potential dangers of a restricted form of government. He placed the future of the state in the hands of the people. In placing the instrument for the welfare of the community in the people Andreae was first obliged to stress the role of education. Utilizing education as one of his main techniques to improve the state and to help it realize its destiny Andreae had to create a new philosophy of education. He hoped to remove dull, repetitive, pedantic and stultifying elements from his proposed school system. Andreae was among the first to attempt to erect a school system that would educate the whole man; he proposed a system of education that was essentially dynamic and practical. Each student was to be fitted for life. The role of the school was to develop the physical qualities along with vocational and domestic skills, moral discipline, social skills and lastly the perceptive powers.

Andreae has proposed, in his *Christianopolis,* many radical ideas which were related to man's social, economic, and political life. The ideal state that he envisaged was deeply concerned with the good of the citizens. Andreae stated that the most important single agency within the state was education. The chief role of education was to produce cultured, free citizens. Freedom implied economic independence, policial choice, moral self-direction, as well as the right to make independent decisions.

The curriculum in the *Christianopolis* was compulsory and

rigid. Each student had to take the sequence of courses offered in the humanities and sciences. Andreae naively felt he had devised the perfect curriculum and he would not permit the students to choose courses. He ignored individual differences and, for example, would not tolerate an elective system in order to promote his idea of the perfect citizen.

Economic independence was assured by requiring that each student should take vocational education courses. Professional schools offered work leading to specialization in medicine, law, nursing, and pharmacy. The over-all attitude presented in the *Christianopolis is* one of dignity and honor and work. Status was not based upon one's employment, but rather upon one's moral and intellectual attainments.

It was imperative that each citizen be engaged actively in determining governmental policies. Andreae proposed that in his free society each person was to take courses in political science in order that they might participate in an intelligent manner.

The motivation for right behavior, Andreae insisted, must come from the individual himself. Character education is, in the main, the development of a sense of responsibility toward God, one's community, and one's self. As a guide to character development, courses were included in the schools. Tablets throughout the city illustrated the virtues and religious teachings. Community worship incited people's religious spirit. However, Andreae insisted, that man must participate religiously as well as in other spheres of activity, always as a member of a group. He denied the individual the right of contemplation from whence comes the great well-spring of strength needed to live according to one's moral convictions.

The school system proposed by Andreae rested upon the premise that education must produce citizens who not only were adept in the humanities, but in the sciences as well.

Psychologically sound principles of sense involvement were basic to his method of teaching.

Audio-visual materials and methods were an integral part of the schools; laboratories, libraries, museums, gardens, and art studies were utilized in daily instruction.

Andreae's genius was reflected in his attempts to put them into practice during his lifetime. The proof of the inherent practicality of his concepts lies in the integration of his concepts in the modern school system. Andreae was an idealist, an optimist who was inspired by a deep religious faith. The fundamental Christian idea of faith, hope, and charity permeated his work and thus the *Christianopolis* is one of the most religious of all utopias.

chapter six

THE NATURE OF THE CONCEPT IN THE *NEW ATLANTIS*

MANY PHILOSOPHERS and scientists of the late fifteenth and early sixteenth centuries felt that Aristotelianism offered intellectual restrictions and consequently they desired a new method with which to investigate nature. Francis Bacon in the *New Atlantis* proposed a new system for the investigation of natural phenomena and initiated the modern tradition of empiricism and utilitarianism.

Bacon was born in 1560 into a family that possessed wealth and position. His father was Lord Keeper of the Royal Seal. Bacon entered Cambridge at the age of twelve, and matriculated in the school of liberal arts. He completed his studies at Cambridge and then went to London where he pursued the study of law. He entered the ranks of those persons engaged in state services, and under Elizabeth and James I he progressed to the highest state offices until he was dishonorably dismissed in 1621. During his retirement he spent his time in study, experimentation and writing. He considered his life-work to be an attempt to dispossess Aristotle as the seer of science and to replace this great prophet by setting up a new system of philosophical inquiry.

The *New Atlantis* consisted largely of a proposed curriculum which rested basically upon Bacon's outline and plan for science. This utopia is the fruition of Bacon's succinct description of his philosophy—knowledge is power.

Philosophy of Education

Bacon felt, as all the utopists did, that the improvement of society could only take place when men gained sufficient knowledge. Bacon devoted his energies to the advancement of the philosophy of education, to developing and perfecting a method of inquiry.

Bacon's first basic premise was that knowledge would solve all social problems. Though this attitude is somewhat naive Bacon attempted to utilize the schools in the solution of human problems.[1] The search for knowledge was the chief concern of all the citizens in the New Atlantis. He called the college ". . . the very eye of the kingdom of New Atlantis."[2] He said that there was no other activity in the state that was as important as the pursuit of knowledge which took place at the college. The role of the university was ". . . to determine the knowledge of causes, the secret motions of things; and the enlarging of the bounds of human knowledge, to the effecting of all things possible."[3]

Bacon believed that knowledge must be disseminated not only to all menbers of the kingdom, restricted only by the ability to learn, but promoted throughout the world. Thus Bacon was among the first to attempt to eliminate the narrow provincial attitude of the scholars of his time who held to the superiority of their knowledge. Bacon singled out in particular the Scholastics as representative of overspecialization and unwillingness to exchange ideas. Bacon stated that the community of scholars in the New Atlantis exchanged ideas with other countries regarding ". . . the sciences, arts, manufactures and inventions, all new books, instruments, and patterns in every kind, and of the affairs of state."[4]

Bacon attempted to break from the Aristotelian-Scholastic tradition first of all by stating that knowledge must not be concerned with final causes, but only with efficient and formal causes.[5]

The state of New Atlantis was essentially a community of scholars—every person learning and contributing what he could to the general fund of knowledge. The method of inquiry in the pursuit of knowledge was Bacon's major contribution to the history of ideas. Bacon proposed an elaborate system of scientific discovery, the inductive method. Science for him was essentially a co-operative enterprise by scholars that utilized all the departments and facilities of the college. Research and publication was the fundamental role of the university. Bacon stressed empiricism and experimentation in his method of inquiry. He was concerned primarily with the study of nature and of human nature, and in particular group dynamics.

Bacon differed from his utopian predecessors in regard to the use of the home as an educational agency. Plato and Campanella made the state an educational institution primarily by means of the elimination of the family.[6] Bacon felt that the home should train the child in character education and moral growth. Obedience and piety were to be taught by the parents. The schools had no responsibility in teaching character education. Though the role of the home in character education was basic, Bacon mistakenly ignored the role of the school in this matter. Loyalty to the state was inculcated at an early period in the life of the child. Civic responsibility was also solely taught in the home where the parents taught the child civil obedience.

The Nature of the Curriculum in the New Atlantis

Bacon proposed a system of course-study that was aimed at developing the potential of each student. Bacon adhered to utopian tradition and constructed a curriculum that would develop the whole man. However, he was not consistent with his avowed aim. The course content of the school system in the New Atlantis was based upon more extensive course work in the area of science than in any other discipline. As a point of fact courses in languages and the humanities were a minor part of the curriculum.

The science division was the most important area in the school according to Bacon. Unlike his utopian predecessors (and subsequently Rousseau), Bacon did not consider the Western heritage and in particular the classical writings as being important in designing a curriculum. Bacon's proposed cirriculum was consistent with his educational philosophy which stated in effect that knowledge must be practical; therefore, the *New Atlantis* contained the most descriptive and original list of new courses in the area of science ever offered to that time.

Bacon divided the department of science into four main divisions: (1) zoology, (2) botany, (3) physics and chemistry, and (4) geology. The function of the department of science was primarily research.

The division of zoology, said Bacon, included courses in ornithology, histology, embryology, microbiology, parasitology, genetics, and herpetology. Courses were offered in hydroponics, agriculture, and grafting under the heading of botany. The main purpose of the department of botany, said Bacon, was to produce new types of plants, and to speed up the growing time and to increase the yield of existing types of plants. In addition to courses in physics and chemistry, courses were offered in meteorology, thermodynamics, spectroscopy, mechanical arts, aeronautics, acoustics and astronomy. The last area, geology, included courses that were essentially practical and were an adjunct to the botany department. They were: petroleum geology, gems and gem materials, sedimentation and stratiography.

A medical college was planned by Bacon. The work of the institution was basically to find means and techniques to improve health and curb disease. A germ-free laboratory was proposed, an an adjunct to microbiology, in the study of disease.

A course comparable to modern social psychology was introduced by Bacon in his curriculum and this new science dealt primarily with experimentation in human behavior. Bacon felt that every phenomenon could be studied and the laws of its behavior could be made known and consequently manipulated by his new science. Thus he offered the subject of social psychology, which dealt with the laws of social behavior; its purpose—the manipulation of groups in such a manner that the best society would emerge. Bacon did not indicate that there were to be any moral injunctions as to the limits the social scientists could transgress in their construction of group behavior.

The girls were required to take courses in home economics and the course included the study of food preparation, child management, clothing construction, nutrition, experimental cooking and baking. Bacon attempted to teach home economics under scientific conditions and therefore utilized laboratories. Experiments were constantly performed with the intent to improve the existing method of food preparation and the construction of clothing, or to introduce variety. The women of New Atlantis were encouraged to view household duties as a vitally important function which insured the welfare of their families and subsequently that of the state; the study of home duties on the college level was planned to help encourage this attitude.

Bacon included courses in grammar and composition and foreign languages in the department of humanities. However, it is evident from Bacon's emphasis on the nature of the science curriculum, and his mere passing reference to the liberal arts, that science was to be the main study in his schools. Further is was the only hope for the solution of human problems. Bacon in the utopian tradition stated his belief that the school must educate the whole man, but the curriculum which he proposed indicated that his school program was inconsistent with his stated belief.

Audio-Visual Methods and Materials

Bacon was committed to the proposition that education must utilize all the senses. He believed that if he were to produce the high level of creativity which he had proposed for his scholars, then opportunities would have to be present for direct sense-experiences, for example, manipulation of materials. He attempted to utilize laboratories and field trips in the teaching of every subject in the science curriculum. He naively assumed that there were no opportunities for the use of audio-visual materials in the liberal arts.

Laboratories were essential in the teaching of science, declared Bacon, because they permitted the study of data maintained under controlled conditions. Bacon used, for example, laboratories that utilized wind tunnels, acoustical chambers, ovens and refrigerators, and telescopes in his study of physics.[7]

Caves and artificial mines were used in the study of geology. Soil and rock specimens were present in each geological classroom. The buildings were surrounded by lakes which contained both fresh and salt water, which were used by students of geology as well as by students of ichthyology.

Extensive gardens abounded in New Atlantis. Every known variety of tree, herb, bush, and grass was grown in orchards next to the botanical gardens. The gardens and orchards served as a place for experimentation in speeding up the growth of plants and trees as well as means of cultivating new types.

Zoos were propounded by Bacon not only as localities which housed unusual and rare types of animals, but also where breeds could undergo experimentation for improvement. Animals anatomically similar to man, for example, apes, were raised in the zoos which insured a ready source of these animals for use in dissection in the medical school.

Bacon felt that rooms should be provided wherein artificial storms—including hail, rain and snow—could be reproduced for the advancement of the study of meteorology.

Bacon, though unacquainted with the germ theory, had some insight into the cause of disease; he stated that the study of medicine utilized one laboratory that was germ-free. The germ-free laboratory was used to carry on experimentation in the cure and prevention of disease. Bacon was convinced that refrigeration would preserve certain materials. Laboratories that contained facilities for refrigeration were also part of the medical school.

The school of home economics and mechanical arts also used laboratories and workshops for experimentation and for means of improvement. Large botanical gardens and enclosures were used by the school of home economics as sources of experimentation with new types of grains and new strains of wheat.

Bacon was very much interested in the study of psychology and proposed that psychology be taught as a laboratory subject. Laboratories utilizing instruments related to the senses, for example, sound, sight and smell, were included by Bacon to delude human senses in order to understand how persons get sense impressions.

Bacon's concern for the utilization of audio-visual materials in his new school system was reflected in the placement of the audio-visual department under the direction of three men who functioned directly under the director of the school system. The function of this group was not only to supervise the audio-visual materials, but also to develop new materials and methods.

Bacon stated that this group would work with the various schools and colleges and assist them in devising applicable materials.

Bacon has enlarged upon a utopian theme in the *New Atlantis*. This theme states in effect that the ears are not the only means, or the best means, of learning. He felt that the other senses of sight, taste, and touch must be utilized in instruction and his position was emphasized in the *New Atlantis* that learning, at least in the sciences, must utilize laboratories, field trips, and other sources of audio-visual materials and methods.

The *New Atlantis* contained several ideas that have in part influenced modern educational practices. Bacon saw clearly that the changing social and intellectual conditions of his time must necessarily be accompanied by innovations in the educational practices. He felt that the new social order he was proposing must have as its single most important agency a school system that would provide philosophy, direction, and goals for man. Thus, in the *New Atlantis*, Bacon proposed what has come to be actualized as a university. The university as proposed by Bacon was the center of culture for the state, but more than that, it was the agency of a coordinated approach to the solution of human ills. Bacon stated that if the university emphasized the role of the sciences it could accomplish many things. A few of the accomplishments of modern universities which Bacon predicted are: curing of diseases, prolongation of life, relief of pain, improvement of species of plants and animals, the use of hypnotism in medicine, improvements in soil and seeds, creation of new types of threads and materials, acceleration of germination and growth of plants, and new types of foods.

Bacon incorporated suggestions for a large, general, scientific library, botanical gardens, laboratories and museums. Modern universities generally have followed Bacon's proposals. However, the first immediate actualization of his idea of a university was in the founding of the Royal Society of London.[8] Modern scientific societies stem from Bacon's *New Atlantis*.

Bacon conceived several new subjects as part of the curriculum of the university. Bacon devised the science of social psychology because he felt that society could only function well if it was administered scientifically. Microbiology was proposed for the first time by Bacon as a scientific study of microscopic life utilizing microscopes and germ-free laboratories and is now a basic course in the science curriculum of modern colleges. Other courses outlined by Bacon included parasitology and hydroponics. Hydroponics has since become a serious study in accordance with population growth because of its possible alternative to soil crops as a source of much of the world's food.

Bacon is perhaps most renowned for the reconstruction of man's attitude toward himself, the world, and ultimately toward God; for as Whitehead stated, "Bacon remains as one of the great builders who constructed the mind of the modern world."[9]

Bacon's first step in the development of his rationale was the removal of final causes. He proposed a system of free scientific inquiry unhampered by teleological questions of good and bad and concerned primarily with the progress of mankind as a whole.[10] In part the *New Atlantis* was an attempt at solving the problems of education by means of the inductive method. John Dewey stated that Bacon's educational reforms, which he said emphasized the struggle for freedom of action and inquiry, were responsible in part for modern epistemology.[11] The basic aspect of Bacon's attitude toward the world was practical; the inductive method as outlined in the *New Atlantis* was the forerunner of modern pragmatism. Dewey stated:

> When William James called Pragmatism a New Name for an Old Way of Thinking, I do not know that he was thinking expressly of Francis Bacon, but so far as concerns the spirit and atmosphere of the pursuit of knowledge, Bacon may be taken as the prophet of a pragmatic conception of knowledge.[12]

While Bacon's inductive method emphasized the practical consequence of knowledge, it also promoted the role of the individual as being fundamental. Bacon stated that all learning, regardless of the fact that it may have been true, must have been tested by the personal experience of the individual before it was true for him.

Summary and Conclusions

Bacon, in the *New Atlantis* moved away from Plato's idea of the philosopher-king (that is a man of universal knowledge ruling the state), and substituted rule by specialists and technicians. Bacon's solution to the *raison d'etre* of utopian writing —social justice—was to propose a country based upon freedom and justice for all citizens. As a utopist Bacon believed that human nature was capable of becoming magnanimous given the right social, political and economic setting. He proposed a reform in the structure of society based upon the laws deduced by scientific inquiry into human society and aided by the improvement of material goods through the exploitation of nature by science. Bacon didn't particularly emphasize education, rather he saw it as a means to an end—the end being the perfect state erected upon the principles of science. The *New Atlantis* was included in this study but it doesn't have the force of the other utopias, since education was not the basic agency of the state. The primary purpose of the college was research rather than teaching. Bacon desired to promote scientific research. Bacon was the most important exponent of the modern era of science.[13] However, his enthusiasm over the possibilities of science led him to excesses. He felt that science alone could perfect human nature and build the perfect world. He was directly responsible for laying the framework for what has become the cult of science. Further, by denying the role of final causes, partially as a benighted attack upon Aristotle, Bacon in part denied man the use of philosophy to aid science in solving social problems. His naive faith in science and his dislike of scholasticism prompted Bacon to ignore the western tradition, both biblical and classical. For example, the school curriculum proposed by Bacon was virtually exclusively scientific, unrelieved and unsupported by the classical writings, for example, More's curriculum in the *Utopia.*

Though Bacon was limited by his adherence to science as the wherewithal of human endeavors he was able, by virtue of his position as a Renaissance scholar and prophet of modern thought, to promote the ideal of security, comfort, health, and dignity in life.

In order to promote social justice by means of scientific advancement Bacon introduced the concept of a state-supported university which was dedicated to experimental science. Other utopists advocated a communal life based upon material possessions, but Bacon proposed a communal life of knowledge. The government was instituted to insure the welfare of the people and Bacon stated that this could only come about if knowledge were free and available to all citizens. The state of New Atlantis became an educational institution in the utopian tradition. The utopists have repeatedly argued that education was the most important agency within the state. Bacon was no less an advocate of the role of education. His emphasis upon providing audio-visual materials and senses in education was an example of his concern in the improvement of education. He believed that coordinated activities of the university held the solution of human progress. He was committed to the proposition that men discovering the truth would automatically become free. The *New Atlantis* was basically an attempt to promulgate Bacon's thesis that the pursuit of truth could be accomplished by means of the advancement of science.

chapter seven

THE NATURE OF THE CONCEPT IN THE *SOCIAL CONTRACT* AND THE *EMILE*

JEAN JACQUES ROUSSEAU was the last writer of a major utopia. To a large extent his political writings helped produce the French Revolution, while in the area of education many of his ideas have been applied and accepted. His two utopias, the *Emile* and *Social Contract,* while concerned with different topics, are supplemental to the central problem of education. It is virtually impossible to understand one without having read the other.

Rousseau was born in 1712 in Geneva, Switzerland. His mother died in childbirth and this occurrence he felt was the beginning of his many troubles. He was reared by his father, who like Jean Jacques was highly sentimental, imaginative, and overly sensitive. In the evenings he and his father often read the sentimental and romantic novels characteristic of the period. Jean Jacques also read Plutarch's *Lives* at a very early age.

During the period of his tenth to his sixteenth year, he lived with a Calvinist minister, was apprenticed to an engraver, and finally ran away because his master subjected him to beatings. He moved to Savoy where he met a Catholic priest who fed him and discussed theology with him. Rousseau decided to become a Catholic. When he was sent to Annacy, a nearby town, to meet Madame de Warens he had expected to meet an old lady, but to his surprise she turned out to be twenty-eight years old and good-looking. Even though he was eighteen at the time he called her "mother," and she called him her "little one!" Rousseau spent nine years with her and during this time he persuaded her to purchase a farm. This period had a great effect upon him, and he spent most of his time walking around the farm and reading. He left Madame de Warens for awhile and upon his return he found a rival installed. He then left for a teaching position as tutor to small children. He spent a very disagreeable year with them and left. This was the extent of his teaching experience.

He moved to Paris where he was entertained and supported by many women due to his good looks and endearing ways. There he met Therese le Vasseur, who appears to have had a very low intelligence. She could not count money or tell time. However, Rousseau spent thirty-five years with her and from this union they had at least five children. As each child was born it was sent to an orphanage.

When he was thirty-seven years old an incident occurred which changed the course of his life. On the way to visit Diderot, who was imprisoned for writing books unpopular with the government, Rousseau saw the announcement of an essay contest sponsored by the Academy of Dijon. The subject was "Has the progress of the arts and sciences contributed to the corruption or to the purification of morals?" The topic impressed him deeply. He wrote an essay taking the position that the arts and sciences had corrupted morals and mankind. Rousseau won the contest and the idea of the noble savage came into existence.

He became famous. He moved to the country and in the cottage where he lived with Theresa he was able to capture the security he remembered from his time with Madame de Warens. During this period he wrote the *New Heloise,* the *Social Contract,* and the *Emile.*

The parliament of Paris declared *Emile* subversive and decreed that the book should be burned and Rousseau hanged. Instead of receiving acclaim and awards he was forced to flee the country.

The last sixteen years of his life were spent in fear and poverty. He died on July 2, 1778, at the age of sixty-six and was buried in the Pantheon next to Voltaire.

Rousseau's Plan for the Improvement of the Human Community

Bacon by means of the inductive method was responsible for the philosophical basis which developed into the concept of the sovereignty of the individual; it remained for Rousseau to present an elaborate plan for the improvement of the human community utilizing this concept. An additional and correlated problem confronted Rousseau immediately, the problem of educating the sovereign citizens so that they could reach their potentiality within the state.

Rousseau wrote the *Emile* at the same time that he wrote the *Social Contract*. The works are closely related, each dealing with different aspects of the same problem, the essential liberty of natural man which should be safeguarded by education—and protected by the lawmaker.

Rousseau began the *Social Contract* with this basic statement:

> The social order is a sacred right which serves as a foundation for all others. This right, however, does not come from nature. It is therefore based upon convention.[1]

The two ideas in the above quotation, that man can only reach his potentiality in civil society, and that each individual must retain his sovereignty while a member of the state, are the core of Rousseau's philosophy.

Rousseau viewed, with some nostalgia, the state of nature, wherein man belonged only to himself. However, Rousseau stated emphatically in both the *Emile* and *Social Contract* that the state of nature was only an intellectual construct and never to be taken as a real condition to which man could aspire; human society was man's rightful heritage. Freedom was the essential ingredient of the state of nature that moved Rousseau. He posed the question in this manner, "How can men live in society, obey the laws of the state, and still retain personal freedom?" Since freedom may be defined as the privilege of following the dictates of one's conscience the solution for Rousseau became simply to have each man follow the law that he was in part responsible for inaugurating. Only by becoming an active and intelligent citizen could each person attain self-direction. Rousseau realized that if sovereignty was to reside in the people and not in the government each citizen would have to take an active role in governing. The uncompromising nature of Rousseau's concept of democracy would never permit the delegation of authority by the people to the state. The general will of the people should be the governing agency.

In Book II of the *Social Contract* Rousseau, in speaking of the inalienable and indivisible sovereignty of the people, stated that if all the people discussed together the results would be efficacious.[2]

Each man must speak out his opinion. It necessarily followed that each man must have knowledge and virtue; this is the role of education for Rousseau.

Self-direction is the keynote of Rousseau's works, for if good government is self-government good citizens are self-directed citizens.

Rousseau's Philosophy of Education

Rousseau's philosophy of education was derived principally from his belief that education must deal with life, and that it must be practical.

> "Life is the trade I will teach my pupil," Rousseau said. "When he leaves me he will not be trained in any occupation, but he will be a man. The real object of our study is man and his environment. True education consists less in precept than in practice. We begin to learn when we begin to live."[3]

In the *Emile* Rousseau presented in part a synthesis of the ideas of some of his utopian predecessors, notably Plato, St. Augustine and Bacon. However, in the main the *Emile*, while original, is a lengthy and inconsistent presentation of Rousseau's inconsistencies, contradictions, and naivete which have been ignored and the truly fine and original ideas have been extracted for incorporation into modern pedagogical practices.

It is altogether fitting that Rousseau, who was in part responsible for the French Revolution, should propose a revolutionary philosophy of education. The term revolutionary may be applied to Rousseau's work in two ways, the first dealing with his original ideas, and the second with his notion that education must be prepared to operate in a period of political and social upheaval. Thus, a reason for the acceptance of his ideas was the fact that he proposed ideas that agreed with the temper of the times.[4]

In terms of the educational ideas proposed by Rousseau the most revolutionary of all was the concept that education must be based upon a study of the whole, natural child.

The first dictum Rousseau presented was that education must train the senses; it must give to the student a knowledge of natural objects and forces.

Thus a basic condition of Rousseau's theory of education was that learning must come about by experience.[5]

Rousseau presented a detailed method of structuring situations that would enable the student to have the right types of experiences, for obviously there must be some means and standard for selecting the proper and educative experiences from the student's social milieu. Learning by means of experience necessitated a peculiar type relationship between the studnt and the teacher. Rousseau's solution to this problem was unrealistic. The tutor spent his whole life with only one student.[6] The teacher controlled the environment completely, even to the extent of practicing deceit to structure the learning situation.[8] One example of a learning-through-experience situation involved the nature of property rights; Rousseau allowed the pupil to plant some beans in a seed bed previously prepared by the gardener. The gardener, upon perceiving the sprouting beans among his Maltese melons, tore out the beans. Rousseau stated that the pupil would immediately perceive that there are certain property rights, gained by labor and possession. Rousseau failed to see that the student might blame him and dislike him for not telling him ahead of time that there were watermelons planted in that area.

Rousseau, in writing the *Emile*, made it quite clear that he was not proposing merely formal rules of learning and behavior, but was giving rules of existence which must be appreciated for their practical and spiritual value. They were variations of the single theme, which so constantly recurred in his writings, to live in keeping with our true nature. The culmination of Rousseau's ideas was the development of his idea of good taste.

Each of the utopian writers selected a single, central idea around which he constructed his system. For Plato it was justice; for More it was the pursuit of pleasure; Campanella sought economic security; Andreae found it in Christianity; Bacon saw science as the center of his system; for Rousseau it was naturalism, but naturalism developed along specific lines, that is, to the level of mature taste.

Rousseau, in his naive deification of the natural man, was faced with the problem of developing an educational program that would produce his desired natural student, but who also would possess the ability to live in the world. Thus, the dilemma presented to Rousseau dealt with the problem of reconciling simplicity with sophistication. Rousseau's solution was his philosophy of taste.

The study of taste naturally followed from the study of sociology. Taste for Rousseau was the development of the power to judge, in the area of morals and social behavior in order to fill one's life with good things, and thus to be happy.[9] Taste was not to be concerned with mundane things:

> "It must be observed," said Rousseau, "that we are not here concerned with what we like because it is serviceable, or hate because it is harmful to us. Taste deals only with things that are indifferent to us, or which affect at most our needs; taste is not required to judge of these, appetite only is sufficient."[10]

Taste was also relative, for ". . . taste has local rules which make it dependent upon the country we are in."[11]

However, there existed certain fundamental rules that applied to taste. The first law, Rousseau was quick to state, was that taste was not general; that is, the vast majority of people had poor taste. The reason for the aboundance of poor taste was that fashion and fads destroyed taste. The models of good taste were to be found in nature. Clothing styles, for example, that bound the body and restricted movements were contrary to the dictates of good taste and nature, which required free and unhampered physical movement on the part of the individual.[12] It was therefore self-evident that luxury and bad taste would be inseparable. Rousseau stated it thus:

> Luxury acquires power and makes us love what is rare and costly; this so-called beauty consists, not in following nature, but in disobeying her. Wherever taste is lavish, it is bad.[13]

It was also axiomatic for Rousseau that good taste implied good morals. The lavish ostentation which was implicit in bad taste produced corruption of the moral life by having created artificial pleasures and which demanded over-stimulation of the sensual. Contrived stimulation, evidenced in society, particulary in the area of sexual behavior, was a necessary concomitant to the abandonment of the way of nature. Once a social group, either primary or secondary, permits luxury and ostentation, it no longer becomes a matter of merely condoning bad taste it *de facto* deifies it. The corruption of what was one simple and good becomes the object of the highest regard by the elite group. An inherent danger recognized by Rousseau was that the subordinate social groups would attempt to surpass the elite group in excesses. Excess, elaboration, and stimulation were related to the luxurious living of the upperclasses; envy and emulation was the role of the lower classes; immorality and unhappiness the inevitable consequences for all groups.

Rousseau proposed a solution. He initiated a specific educational program that would produce good taste. Students who trained in this program need not have retired to simple cultures in order to pursue good taste. They could live, said Rousseau, even in that haven of bad taste, Paris, and still not be corrupted.

Rousseau found in the classics a basis for his program to develop pure and wholesome taste. Rousseau agreed with More in establishing the classics as the keystone of the curriculum. Rousseau said that the incorporation of the books which have withstood the test of time was fundamental because:

> There is certain simplicity of taste which goes straight to the heart; and this is only to be found in the classics. In oratory,

> poetry, and every kind of literature, Emile[14] will find the classical authors as he found them in his study of history, full of matter and sober in their judgment.[15]

Rousseau has been criticized because, it is asserted, he relied completely, in his theory of learning, upon the technique of discovery.[16] This is, however, not the case, for while Rousseau did emphasize the role of discovery in learning he was emphatic in praising the value of ancient and accumulated learning.

Rousseau insisted that the classics for some students should be original Latin and Greek.[17] He gave no reason for this idea.

Rousseau felt that the student would have a deep love for the classics, and would learn more from them concerning, among other things, the nature of good taste; however, he also permitted the student to read modern literature if for no other reason than to reaffirm his judgment in the superiority of the classics.[18]

From the study of the classics Rousseau hoped his student would learn to love beauty, which, he said, was the foundation of good taste. However, to insure the development of good taste it was necessary to align the student's intellectual growth closely to nature. Good taste for Rousseau was essentially a habit—a habit which resulted in choosing suitable, beneficial, and moral pleasures.[19]

Good taste operated in all areas of human activity.[20] Good taste was the result of the proper type of education and it produced the truly happy individual, that is, the individual in harmony with nature. Rousseau summarized his philosophy of taste succinctly:

> Let our tastes change with our years, let us no more meddle with age than with the seasons. We should be ourselves at all times, instead of struggling against nature; such vain attempts exhaust our strength and prevent the right use of life.[21]

Rousseau proposed educational goals that were far-reaching in scope; he hoped his system of natural education would make man free, productive and morally good. In the *Emile* and *Social Contract* Rousseau offered for consideration specifically the following aims: civic competence, vocational orientation, preparation for family living, and health and physical fitness.

Rousseau's Psychology of Education

Rousseau's educational psychology, closely related to his philosophy of education, has been one of the major forces in contemporary pedagogical theory and practice.

The *Emile* is, from a purely technical aspect, rambling, discursive, and lacking in internal organization; however, the main plan of the work conformed closely to Rousseau's concept of periods in the psychological development of the personality. The over-all plan of the *Emile* was to have each chapter conform to a developmental period. Rousseau presented within each chapter the data by which he attempted to demonstrate his principles relating to the psychological phenomena underlying his system of education. The categorization of psychological phenomena according to stages has validity; however, Rousseau overemphasized the periods of mental growth. He either failed to recognize, or simply ignored the fact that mental growth is developmental and evolutionary and not characterized by end-stop stages unrelated either to the preceding or subsequent stage.

The first stage of personality development according to Rousseau comprised the period between birth and two years of age. Within each developmental period Rousseau attempted to promote at least one major aspect of mental development that would make the period unique. In defining the need-structure of the infant, Rousseau said that love was crucial to the child's development. Rousseau's statement regarding the role of love was contradictive because he was unwilling to explore the consequences of his position regarding nature. An example of romantic overemphasis was Rousseau's statement regarding the natural role of the mother in feeding:

> When mothers deign to nurse their own children, then there will be a reform in morals; natural feeling will revive in every heart; there will be no lack of citizens for the state; this first step by itself will restore mutual affection.[22]

Love is a major force in personality development at any stage; it is specifically important in the early formative years. In recognizing this fact Rousseau made a major contribution which Freud a hundred years later presented to the world as original. However, Rousseau contradicted himself by demanding that the infant also be raised in a stoic environment.

> "This is nature's law," said Rousseau. "Why contradict it? Accustom infants to the hardships they will have to face; train them to endure extremes of temperature, climate, and condition, hunger, thirst, and weariness.[23]

Rousseau was inconsistent in his attempts to promulgate a parallel system of love and stoicism in rearing children. However, the depth of his insights and the fervor with which he presented them, for example, in detailing the minutest aspect of nursery life, indicated a genuine interest in the good and sanctity of childhood. In his precepts for the proper care of children, Rousseau emphasized breast feeding, loose and comfortable clothes, absolute freedom of movement, and proper ventilation.[24]

Rousseau attempted to imbue his audience with a fear of fear. He was insistent that the child should never know fear. Rousseau presented an elaborate set of devices and advice regarding control the parents should utilize in structuring the child's environment so the fear-producing situations and events would be virtually eliminated.[25] Rousseau also composed a system of discipline that was not based upon the element of fear, that is, by having the punishment result as a natural consequence of a wrong act.

Rousseau assumed that the fundamental law of nature was that strength had survival power; and while he was cognizant of the fact that education must "denature" man in order for society to exist, he continued to pursue the idea that strength was important. Rousseau said:

> All wickedness comes from weakness. The child is only naughty because he is weak; make him strong and he will be good; if we could do everything we should never do wrong.[26]

Possibly the most important aspect of the infant's personality development is the progression from the state of a young animal to that of a member of society. Rousseau would have the child learn to surrender part of his personal liberty, and to understand that this partial surrender need not entail unhappiness. This would be accomplished by a gradual process of education. Rousseau emphasized the fact that this process of rational introduction to socialization could not begin too early; actually he said it must begin before the child learned to talk.

Summing up his rules for this first personality-epoch Rousseau said:

> The spirit of these rules is to give children more real liberty and less power, to let them do more for themselvse and demand less of others.[27]

The period between two years of age and twelve was considered by Rousseau to be the second personality-epoch. This is the stage of negative education. Here, said Rousseau, we must lose time in order to gain it.[28] What did he mean by this seeming paradox? In point of fact Rousseau actually glorified idleness during this period; however, there are many elements of value for a progressive psychology of learning. To begin with Rousseau said:

> Nature would have them children before they are men. If we try and invert this order we shall produce fruit immature and flavorless, fruit which will be rotten before it is ripe . . . treat the student according to his age.[29]

Once the point had been established that children were not miniature adults it was possible to deduce the laws of mental growth that were relative to them. The laws pertaining to children to the age of twelve, said Rousseau, were based upon the principles of negative education.

> The child should be brought to the age of twelve strong and healthy, but unable to tell his right hand from his left. He should be free from prejudices and habits. Leave childhood to ripen in children. In a word, beware of giving anything they need today if it can be deferred without danger to tomorrow.[30]

Rousseau resolved the paradox by stating that he realized students would not be brought up in complete isolation.

Rousseau wanted this "waste of time" to take place in the state of nature. The major skills developed by students during this period fall in the general category of "scoutcraft." Since Rousseau held that education was made for the child and not contrariwise the needs and the interests of the child were of paramount importance in determining the content of his education.

The basic need-structure of the child, said Rousseau, must be kept simple. The teacher must have a definite ability to be able to determine "real" needs from peripheral, socially induced needs. Rousseau said:

> The surest way to make a child miserable is let him have everything he wants; for as his wants increase in proportion to the ease with which they are satisfied, the teacher will be compelled, sooner or later, to refuse his demands, and this unlooked-for refusal will hurt him more than the lack of what he wants.[31]

In addition Rousseau said, "Nature has made children helpless and in need of love, but she did not make them to be obeyed and feared."[32]

Children rebel if their felt needs are frustrated, but Rousseau was adamant that punishment should not be capricious or arbitrary but should be a natural consequence of the act. Thus in a particularly naive example he proposed that a student who breaks a window should be required to sleep in the room containing the damaged glass.

The role of interests incorporated several secondary considerations, among which the most important was the ability of the child to rationalize his interests. The problem of knowledge for Rousseau hinged in part upon the nature of language. Rousseau considered the intellectual abilities of students in the two to twelve year group to be severely limited. He said:

> Of all man's faculties, reason, which is compounded of all the rest, is the last to develop, and cannot be used in children's early training. To make a man reasonable is the coping stone of a good education, and yet some profess to train a child through his reason![33]

For Rousseau an interest could only become actualized upon its being verbalized. The reason children cannot reason is because they have a limited vocabulary. We think with words. Rousseau followed Campanella closely and anticipated modern sematics, and in particular he anticipated Korzybski, Johnson, and Lewin,[34] when he stated that the whole nature of thought was integrally related to language and the meaning of words.[35] Rousseau stated a profound insight in this area when he felt that personality took its unique character from the type of language native to one. He said:

> Every language has its own form, a difference which may be partly cause and partly effect of differences in national character.[36]

A country such as Indonesia whose language does not contain words of precise definition cannot have a scientific development, thus this country will be handicapped in the modern scientific period.

The child during this period, according to Rousseau, was extremely curious. Two problems arose for Rousseau: how to direct this avid curiosity along beneficial lines, and how to keep it within socially approved limits.

The problem of socially approved behavior was vastly oversimplified by Rousseau. He said that the most important ethical lesson for the young student to lear, in order to alleviate distress in his dealings with others, was the nature of property rights. Rousseau naively state: "The first idea a student msut learn is not that of liberty but of property."[37]

Rousseau's belief that property rights were fundamental in social relationships represents on his part a basic break with the utopian tradition of collectivism. Instead he proposed a scheme of violent individualism.

The problem of curiosity was to a large degree the center of Rousseau's psychology of learning. He encouraged teachers to practice deceit in order to utilize curiosity effectively. He said:

> This child, without knowledge, strength or wisdom, is entirely at the teacher's mercy; the teacher is master of the student's

> whole environment. The teacher can make of the student what he pleases. Let the student think he is master while the teacher is really the master.[38]

The role of the teacher in Rousseau's scheme of education was undemocratic. Rousseau artlessly assumed in his Arcadian school that the teacher would always guide the student along lines that were best for him, following, of course, Rousseau's principles. For example, in directing the student's curiosity the teacher could indicate to the student the techniques for controlling desire and thus the student would know how to attain happiness. Rousseau stated:

> True happiness consists in decreasing the difference between our desires and our powers, in establishing a perfect equilibrium between the power and the will.[39]

Rousseau did not believe in the transfer of learning. He stated in general of all learning of this period:

> All knowledge gained on this level is on the sensation-level, nothing penetrates to the understanding. The memory of students under twelve years of age is little better than their other powers, for they always have to learn over again, when they are grown up, what they learnt as children.[40]

Rousseau believed that a child under twelve years of age was, if not immoral, at least amoral. With the exception of property rights Rousseau felt it was impossible to teach the child anything regarding ethical conduct. Only by appealing to the child's strong ego feelings could any positive ethical behavior be produced. In regard to character development Rousseau also applied the principles of negative education. Rather than attempt to inculcate moral habits the teacher should try to shield the child from evil.[41] Rousseau disagreed with Locke's idea of constantly reasoning with children.[42] Because children had no reasoning powers Rousseau would have had the child live in a moral vacuum. It is true that some forms of reasoning are somewhat late in developing. However, Rousseau failed to realize that the process must begin some time, and the sooner the better.

The third personality-epoch consisted of the years between twelve and fifteen. This period, Rousseau felt, comprised the two main events in the student's education: the development of the intellectual powers, and the beginning of vocational education.

Rousseau proposed that upon the student's twelfth birthday his negative education be immediately terminated and suddenly be exposed to positive education. He based this proposal upon Aristotle's faculty psychology, in which he ardently believed, stating[43] in effect that the different faculties of the mind[44] developed at different age periods. Rousseau said in the *Emile*:

> It is impossible to teach sooner than the student is ready and able to understand.[45]

The teacher must wisely determine the level of difficulty and need of the material to be presented to the student. Rousseau said, "Beware of anticipating teaching that which demands more maturity of mind."[46] However, the teacher must be aware of the psychological laws of learning operating during this period of mental growth. Thus, the teacher never forces the student to learn; the teacher merely suggests to the student what he should study, relying upon the student's need and desire to select subject matter. The most important injunction Rousseau levied upon teachers at this stage was to utilize as little as possible the lecture method. He said:

> I do not like verbal explanations. Young people pay little heed to them, nor do they remember them. Things! Things! I cannot repeat it too often. We lay too much stress upon words; we teachers babble, and our scholars follow our examples.[47]

He preferred that students learn from the classics and from nature. Rousseau was inconsistent in that he did not follow his advice concerning over-verbalizing to students.[48] There is great value in realizing and pointing out as he did that spoken injunctions, prohibitions and platitudes are a virtual meaningless substitution for the more meaningful experiences gained by activity, example and visual apprehension.

The last stage of mental growth began at the fifteenth year and ended at the age of twenty. This period, Rousseau felt, should develop the psychological mechanism basic to moral and social conduct.

It was a major error on Rousseau's part to assume that students could not begin to appreciate the laws of moral and social conduct before their fifteenth year; further, the means with which he proposed to teach the rules of conduct were naive.

Rousseau based the whole of his projected ethical system upon what he felt was the basic psychological need of the adult, self-love. Rousseau, at Hobbes, was vitally concerned with human survival. He attempted to justify his emphasis upon this point by saying:

> Self-love is always good, always in accordance with the self order of nature. The preservation of our own life is specially entrusted to each one of us, and our first care is, and must be, to watch over our own life.[49]

Rousseau felt that the need structure could be divided into two areas: (1) basic needs; and (2) peripheral needs. The chief role of education was to give the student the knowledge whereby he could achieve happiness by limiting his peripheral needs, that is, to enable him to live simply and naturally. Rousseau, in grounding his system of education upon his principles of psychology, naturally utilized his theory of needs as the basis for educational proposals. The teacher, said Rousseau, must ever keep in mind the basic need structure of his student and center his material upon it.

Rousseau's analysis of needs is fundamentally shallow. He failed to recognize this fact and attempted to base the laws of moral and social conduct upon it. He said that because the child's basic need is self-love any person who ministers to the child becomes an object of love also.

> "The child's first sentiment is self-love," said Rousseau. "His second, which is derived from it, is love of those about him: for in his state of weakness he is only aware of people through the help and attention received from them."[50]

It was impossible to recognize any form of altruism or charity in Rousseau's idea of psychological motives, because the source of every action was essentially selfish. The basic cement of marriage itself was based upon selfishness, because marriage gratified the sex impulse. The second basic human need said Rousseau was sex. Any person who gratified one's sex needs was automatically loved, according to Rousseau's exaggerated romanticism, because they assisted the person in gratifying his own needs. Thus, the most sublime union between humans—marriage—becomes a mere voluptuous relationship between two independent and detached persons who have struck up a convenient partnership to satisfy certain basic sex drives.

It was impossible for Rousseau to erect any sort of social relationship upon his shallow ideas of selfishness. He was forced to propose some basis for human interaction. Sympathy, he said, was the foundation of all human social relationships. Rousseau presented several naive maxims regarding pity.

> It is not in human nature to put ourselves in the place of those who are happier than ourselves, but only in the place of those who can claim our pity. We never pity another's woes unless we know we may suffer in like manner ourselves. The pity we feel for others is proportionate, not to the amount of the evil, but to the feelings we attribute to the sufferers.[51]

Rousseau has taken one of man's noblest sentiments, sympathy, and degenerated it into selfish pity and upon this pity has attempted to erect a system of moral conduct. Thus, according to Rousseau, the student enters young adulthood with no other source of altruism than a mild form of horror over misfortunes of others, because it may in turn happen to him. Rousseau would have every student enter adulthood without even the rudiments of social conscience.

Rousseau said that the intellect becomes a source of enjoyment for the young adult; he believed that one of the chief duties of education was to teach the student to enjoy himself by himself. This was done by two means: one necessitated teaching the student a trade, the other means was to develop the pleasures of the mind. Rousseau stated that thinking was what he wanted to teach so that students could find happiness in enjoying the pleasures of their mind.[52] Thus the last step in stages of personality-epochs was, for Rousseau, the development of the intellectual powers and of good taste.

While Rousseau attempted to present a detailed account of his ideas concerning personality-epochs, in reality he merely proposed a system of educational psychology that was disorderly and was based upon an idea that children should be considered as mere sensuous beings, controlled by sensuous instincts and not amenable to reason. Rousseau's system of psychology was tainted by romanticism. Rousseau emphasized the sacredness of childhood. He based education upon the needs and interests of the student. He felt adult behavior could be explained on the basis of childhood experiences.

Curriculum

Because of Rousseau's theories regarding educational psychology is was impossible for him to erect a curriculum that was rigid, conforming to schedules and rules rather than to the needs and interests of the child. Rousseau subordinated curriculum to the child. Courses of study existed only in so far as they could aid the student.

However, Rousseau felt that there were some courses that had value, and that students should be exposed to them.

Following Plato he first of all felt organized gymnastics should be engaged in by students. He stated in the *Emile*:

> To learn to think we must exercise our limbs, our senses, and our bodily organs, which are the tools of our intellect; and to get the best use out of these tools, the body which supplies us with them must be strong and healthy. Not only is it quite a mistake that true reason is developed apart from the body, but it is a good bodily constitution which makes the workings of the mind easy and correct.[53]

Among the academic courses Rousseau felt were important was geography. Obviously the world of nature being so important to Rousseau's scheme it was imperative that the student should study it. Following Bacon's inductive method Rousseau would have the student study his known world first.

> "The student's geography," said Rousseau, "must begin with the town he lives in and his father's country house, then the places between them, the rivers near them, and then the sun's aspect and how to find one's way by the sun's aid."[54]

Rousseau included visual-arts instruction in geography. The students had the responsibility of making maps.[55]

Science was included by Rousseau because it was a means to learn the secrets of nature. Rousseau proposed the analytic as well as synthetic method in nature study.[56] He believed strongly in the student performing experiments.

History was studied utilizing the "great man" idea rather than studying events. The reason for this was that Rousseau hoped students would benefit from reading the lives of important individuals. Such books as *Robinson Crusoe* and Plutarch's *Lives* were proposed texts because they indicated how some men overcame great difficulties.

Literature, including the classics, was an important course as has already been indicated, because it helped develop good taste.

Rousseau included two courses in curriculum development: sociology and sex education.

Sociology was first proposed as a serious study by Rousseau.[57] The proper study of mankind necessitated, said he, not mere reliance upon books, but rather scientific observation. Observation required field trips. Rousseau was emphatic in his statements that travel was essential in anthropological studies.[58] Rousseau's insistence upon grounding his pupil in the principles of sociology was based upon his idea that in order for a person to live effectively and happily in society one must know the laws that govern society.

Sex education was first introduced into the mainstream of education by Rousseau in the *Emile*. Rousseau recognized the fact that education, in order to be effective, must be complete. It must educate the whole man. Feeling, as he did, that sex was a basic need, it is axiomatic that students must be given instruction in its functions and obligations.

The first condition Rousseau raised was the personality period in which education should begin. He said as soon as the child became curious about sex he should be introduced to sex education and not be put off with fairy stories or lame excuses.[59] However, he stated, "Let your answers regarding sex to young children be always grave, brief, decided, and without trace of hesitation."[60] Sex education was treated from the standpoint of its physical and mental aspects and was divorced from moral aspects. Rousseau felt that the major control for concupiscence should be by means of the development of modesty. Associated with modesty were controls of nature itself, which Rousseau felt were effective, but which he could not adequately explain except to postulate certain concepts which modern psychology calls sublimation.

The limited number of courses proposed by Rousseau did not imply that these would be all the student would ever study. They were the ones Rousseau felt were most important. He did state that the needs of the child would determine subjects to be studied; for example, an interest in rocks might lead to geology, stars to astronomy, measuring to mathematics. Fundamentally the courses were designed to meet the needs of the child.

Educational Opportunities for Women

Rousseau was not, in the area of female educational opportunities, in the utopian tradition. The weakest and most inconsistent area of his proposed educational reforms was in the area of female education. At no time was he able to overcome his inherent fear of women.[61]

Rousseau stated that, in the main, women were the same as men in regard to similarity of biological needs and intellectual abilities.[62] Actually he said that the women were more like men than they were different. In only one area could he find difference—that of the reproductive system. He ascribed all personality differences to sex differences; thus, men were strong and active, women weak and passive. He stated that women were actually stronger in inter-personal relationships because of man's strong sex drive. He believed that women's supremacy was due to their being sex outlets for men. This attitude was the basis for his whole concept of female education and psychology.

Rousseau was particularly apprehensive of the amount of role-reversal he saw in contemporary France.[63] He felt there was a specific role for women and that education must prepare them for it. He attacked Plato's position regarding the educational, social, and political status of women. This is consistent with Rousseau's stand; Plato was among the very first to elevate the role and dignity of women. Rousseau said:

> Plato, in getting rid of the family, found there was no place for women in his system of government, so he was forced to turn them into men. He gave them the same occupations as men, a scheme which could only lead to intolerable evils.[64]

From the proofs of nature Rousseau drew this conclusion:

> Nature means women to think, to will, to love, to cultivate their minds as well as their persons; she puts these weapons in their hands to make up for their lack of strength and to enable them to direct the strength of men.[65]

The role of women was marriage and motherhood; female education was directed toward this purpose.[66] Women could only be truly happy in their "rightful" role, thus their education had to include the means by which to make their future husbands happy.

The first course in Rousseau's proposed curriculum for women was devoted to making them strong and healthy: it was physical education. However, while gymnastics were primarily used by boys to develop muscles and make them strong, Rousseau wanted physical education to develop grace in girls. "Women should be strong enough," said Rousseau, "to do anything gracefully; men should be skillful enough to do anything easily."[67]

Fundamental to the female curriculum were courses in the home-making arts: cooking, sewing, interior decorating, and child care.[68] Rousseau felt that art and drawing were very important courses for girls, probably because they tend to make girls artistic. Female education, said Rousseau, must be practical, not only because their role was primarily as homemakers, but because they could not grasp the things male minds could. Rousseau's male chauvinism is best indicated in this quotation:

> The search for abstract and speculative truths, for principles and axioms in science, for all that tends to wide generalization, is beyond a woman's grasp; their studies should be thoroughly practical. It is their business to apply the principles discovered by men. A woman's thoughts, beyond the range of her immediate duties, should be directed to the study of men, for the works of genius are beyond her reach.[69]

In the area of religion Rousseau was even more explicit in his undemocratic attitude toward women. He refused women freedom of choice in religious matters. They had to follow their husband's religion.[70]

Rousseau's attitude toward women was purely sensualistic. In essence he regarded them as simple, not existing for their own sake, but for men. Thus it was irrelevant to him if women ever developed and realized their own personality, for the husband molded the wife to his will and desires. Women were, according to Rousseau's scheme, never the equal of men, they were never spiritual beings with full rights and privileges. He was not interested in teaching women to think; therefore, he gave no specific and well-defined course of studies for them.

Rousseau's Principles of Character Education

Character education was important to Rousseau because it was the final development of the qualities that enabled man to live effectively in society.[71] In point of fact character education was a major adjunct to taste. Fundamentally character education for Rousseau meant self-discipline, but not decorum, good taste but not altruism, chastity but not charity, pity but not brotherhood, sympathy but neither faith nor good-works.

Rousseau reiterated the truism that a child cannot benefit from character education or make moral decisions before he can reason. However, Rousseau felt that the ability to reason did not come until about fifteen years of age. Upon reaching the age of reason, Rousseau stated, the basis for ethical education must utilize the mechanism of self-love.[72]

Character education, for Rousseau, was taught in two ways: (1) by example and (2) by reading the great books and by reading the lives of great men, for example, Socrates, Christ, and Plutarch's *Lives.* The student[73] would emulate their deeds and solve problems in the manner of the heroes of history. In summary Rousseau felt that character education was necessarily related to good taste. Good taste incorporated, as one important adjunct, civility as well as aloofness from evil.

Principles of Vocational Education

Rousseau was explicit in his philosophy of vocational education. Every student, regardless of background or anticipated station in life must learn a trade, said Rousseau. Because manual labor is "closest to nature,"[74] the student should choose his basic trade in this area. Rousseau would have each student choose a basic trade in the manual arts to insure employment if he did not succeed in his choice of occupation in the professions.

Farming was Rousseau's first choice among the occupations. Rousseau, as did the preceding utopists, felt that working close to the soil, in the state of nature, was an ennobling experience. It gave man a sense of independence and a feeling of contact with the supernatural. More and Bacon would have each citizen own a garden; Rousseau would have the whole world a garden where each person could wander freely. Regarding farming Rousseau said:

> Agriculture is the earliest, the most honest of trades, and more useful than all the rest, and therefore more honorable for those who practice it.[75]

However, while Rousseau preferred agriculture to other occupations he did not require, as did More, for example, that all students must first of all learn farming; actually he wanted his student[76] to learn any trade in order to be independent if he lost his income, but more important to dispel any prejudice felt toward the working classes.

Rousseau proposed certain criteria for the selection of a job for his student. Female choice was limited to the home arts. For example, a girl might choose to become a tailor, seamstress, nurse, cook, or a teacher. In general, Rousseau would have women choose tasks that were performed indoors, that utilized their special abilities, (for example, the ability to sew), and which required little physical strength. Thus, it was axiomatic that the requirements for male jobs would be that they be performed outdoors and that they require physical exercise. Rousseau stated:

> Give a man a trade befitting his sex, to a young man a trade befitting his age. Sedentary indoor employments, which make the body tender and effeminate, are neither pleasing nor suitable. An unhealthy trade I would forbid my pupil, but not a difficult or dangerous one.[77]

Rousseau felt that each student should be acquainted with the general terms, tools, and functions of most other trades. However, in choosing his trade the student should be motivated by interest and ability.

Rousseau proposed that vocational education would be carried out exclusively by the apprentice method. He was prejudiced against traditional school systems. The idea never occurred to him that schools could teach vocational education.

Rousseau has been called one of the major figures in modern educational reform.[78] He expanded traditional educational ideas, for example, in the area of vocational education, character education, and curriculum development.

The range of his ideas has been great. His ideas have run the gamut of every aspect of education, but perhaps his major contribution has been in the area of the philosophy and psychology of education.

To a large degree modern educational theory is the result of Rousseau's pedagogical ideas. To begin with, his ideas toward the child were revolutionary. His idea that all education must be based upon an experimental knowledge of child psychology has permeated modern educational practice.

The fundamental tenet of Rousseau's philosophy was the sacredness of childhood. Rousseau was able to comprehend this axiom because he was among the first to break away from the Renaissance conception of man as a learning and remembering animal. He saw education not as merely a means to ingrain knowledge and facts but as a technique of imbuing culture, taste, discipline and vocational and civic competence. The purpose of education was to create well-rounded human beings. The denunciation of bookishness and arbitrary methods of discipline that began with Rousseau are accepted theorems of modern education. Modern educational practices accepted Rousseau's major tenet and made it fundamental: education must be progressive. Natural education must be a process of growth and unfolding, to be helped by professional educators but not hampered by them.

In the area of curriculum development Rousseau proposed three courses. The first which was not consistent with his position was the use of the classics in history, literature and in developing character.[79] The second course proposed by Rousseau was sociology. Rousseau stated that the study of sociology was to be treated as a science of human group behavior. Many secondary schools, as well as all colleges, include courses in sociology in their curriculum.

The third course proposed by Rousseau was sex education, including family relationships. There is an acceptance in modern schools of courses dealing with family and sex relationships. Such courses as "Home and Family Living" are taught in many American high schools.

Rousseau had several ideas concerning education that have not been accepted as yet, but which have merit.[80] The first major idea that has not been completely exploited[81] is the movement of the school plant into the outdoors which is not practical in any extensive form, but for some specific groups it offers many advantages. For example, the problem of juvenile delinquency might in part be solved by recourse to outdoor living. The largest percentage of delinquents come from the center of the city, the area of transition, crowded homes and streets. Young boys, as Rousseau so aptly pointed out, have a great deal of energy; in the city there are no outlets for their energy. Even energy that has hostile elements could be controlled in the woods, for example, in cutting down trees. Boredom by routine school practices, or in a job, lack of outlets for creative or physical energies, all contribute to juvenile delinquency. During the depression of 1929-1938 the Federal Government had a program—the Civilian Conservation Corps—for young men. This program took unemployed boys from the cities and put them to work in the Federal and State forests building roads, planting trees, cutting timber, and other conservation work. Many of these camps, abandoned during World War II, still stand. A Federal and State program of matching funds supporting camps along the lines of the CCC program would appear to be an effective means of circumventing the sending of young offenders to overcrowded penal institutions. It would be cheaper and more efficient to use such camps than to build more walled prisons. Further, a large percentage of boys who are not amenable to classroom learning and activities and who are not actually delinquents, but potential delinquents, could be sent to such camps thereby relieving the schools of those students who are discipline problems and who lower the academic level of the class.

A second suggestion, Rousseau made, concerned the area of vocational education. And while Rousseau was overly one-sided in his statements, there is some merit in considering at least, in part, some of his recommendations. Rousseau felt that vocational education should not be carried on in the school, but should be in the form of an apprentice program. He felt that only on-the-job training should be the basis of training in the trades.[82] The problem that needs exploring is whether or not the factory needing the skill might not do a better job than the school. This does not apply to all areas, for example, typing, shorthand, etc. where the job-candidate must know rudimentary skills in order to be considered. There are areas, however, where unnecessary duplication takes place, or where the school uses out-of-date practices that hinder the student in actually performing the job. There are certain practices, different with each manufacturer, that the school could not in its limited time be able to teach. While it is not advocated that all vocational education be removed from the schools, careful re-evaluation of the schools' role in vocation education should be made.

Summary and Conclusions

Rousseau was a writer of profound importance in many fields. For example, Ernst Cassirer referred to him as a major figure in the development of modern aesthetic theory.[83] Babbitt called him the father of the modern novel and play.[84] Rousseau has been called the father of modern liberalism,[85] and Stuart Chase said, "Two bloody revolutions, the American and the French, were found about slogans derived from Rousseau."[86] Rousseau has had a deep effect upon subsequent philosophy. For example, the opening statement of Kant's *Critique of Pure Reason*[87] was derived from the *Emile*.[88] Besides Kant, Rousseau had a direct influence upon Basedow, Pestalozzi, Froebel, and Montessori.[89]

Rousseau conceived of personality growth as taking place in manifestly arbitrary epochs. He divided these epochs into four major stages: (1) the first two years of life; (2) two years to twelve years; (3) twelve years to fifteen years; and (4) fifteen to twenty years of age.

The first period was characterized by a great need for love, and the demand by Rousseau that the child be given complete freedom of movement. The second stage, Rousseau stated, should be dominated by his principles of negative education. Here one gains time by losing it. The child's heart is shielded from vice, and he learns to love the world of nature. The third period was concerned with intellectual education and vocational education. The last stage was dominated by learning moral and social rules of conduct.

In considering the *Emile* it is obvious that it reflects Rousseau's personality.[90]

The *Emile* was proposed by Rousseau to be a realistic case history. However, it is never possible to believe this fact. The book is inconsistent, excessive and iconoclastic. Any system, including that of education, that is proposed should be practical; it should take into consideration the ordinary, mundane, and normal aspects of the average situation. Rousseau did just the opposite. For example, his student would be taught in isolation by a tutor who would spend at least twenty-five years with his student. The tutor was enabled, apparently without the existing presence of parents, to structure the educational situation in order to present learning experiences. Rousseau believed that the student would never be able to see through the teacher's contrived situations. However, Rousseau did see and stressed as being important, that the student must learn consequences, and in the area of discipline he felt that punishment should be a natural consequence of his acts.

Rousseau never was able to realize that the student must become an integral unit of his contemporary social system. He did not realize that freedom was a natural intellectual development that had to exist in an area of choice. He saw the child as a mere sensuous being, and not capable of reasoning. Thus he failed to see a major aspect of education which is to give the child an intellectual basis in order to make right decisions in a moral and rational life. Rousseau, by removing reason and conscience from the student's world, removed the very foundation of the social order into which the child would some day have to participate.

Rousseau's effort to subjugate women and make them an instrument of men was undemocratic and attacked the fundamental premise of not only the utopian tradition, but the whole tradition of the West. In effect the whole system of Rousseau was, at least in the area of education, undemocratic, for he limited his system only to the wealthy and healthy.

By positing the basic motives for social intercourse as mere self-interest he was opposed to the very heart of liberalism. Those such as Chapman,[91] who attempted to paint Rousseau as a liberal, have ignored this fundamental tenet in which he wholeheartedly believed.

It is possible to level many legitimate criticisms at Rousseau, particularly after one hundred and fifty years have elapsed; however, he stands as a major figure in the area of educational reform and the last of the classical utopists. The subsequent stage of utopian writing—the utopian-socialists—derived its impetus and ideas from Rousseau. He terminated one period and began another in the history of ideas. This chapter has dealt with his ideas and contributions in the area of education—Rousseau's major concern.

chapter eight

CONTRIBUTION OF THE CLASSICAL UTOPISTS TO MODERN EDUCATION

THE CLASSICAL UTOPIAS were written not only in the spirit of liberalism, but in a genuine atmosphere and feeling of radicalism.[1] The writers were dissenters and iconoclasts. Utopian beliefs hinged upon the idea that human institutions had failed to promote social justice. Therefore, the utopists felt these institutions would have to be eliminated and replaced by new agencies and modes of living. The reorganization of the political construction of the state was the first proposal each reform writer made. However, each proponent of change felt that education was the primary and efficacious agency in the production of good citizens. Thus, each classical utopist necessarily devoted most of his analysis and presentation to educational reform.

The term classical utopia was meant to convey the idea of a reform scheme that was complete in very detail of human life. This included political, economic, social, and intellectual spheres of activity. It appeared significant that those utopias which were most complete devoted much space to detailed programs of education. Utopian literature in the main has been neglected. The term itself has developed a traditional meaning of unrealistic fantasy. There has been no serious attempt to analyze the concepts contained therein. A study of the classical utopias appears fruitful particularly in the area of education.

The right to dissent has been often denied to men. The utopian writers used a particular form to promote their iconoclastic ideas. Their radicalism was contained under the guise of works of fiction.

The writings of the utopists had several points which were held in common. Each writer was concerned basically with social justice. Because of the inequalities, deficiencies and corruption of the times in which he lived, each utopian was essentially critical of the status quo. But, criticism, per se, may be the property of any intelligent observer. The utopians offered something new. They gave original and optimistic contributions in the area of solutions to the problems confronting mankind. The majority of the reform writers were in the main idealistic and had tremendous faith in the future perfectability of the human race.

The attitude of utopianism, while embodying radicalism and iconoclasm, reflects a strong faith in the perfectability of the human race and an attainment of social justice through social change induced by governmental and educational agencies.

Plato, in the *Republic* was concerned with the problem of justice. The state he proposed was to have sole responsibility in administering justice, which in general meant that every person performed in the occupation to which he was best suited. Education was for Plato the most important institution within the state. Plato initiated certain pedagogical postulates and they included: (1) education should be under the jurisdiction of the central government with the responsibility for the overseeing of the schools given to the minister of education; (2) education should be compulsory; (3) women should have equal rights in education; (4) schools should be divided into primary, secondary, and higher divisions; and (5) schools should be responsible for character education.

The *Republic* was an attempt to insure a rational society. The critical problem of obligation, to oneself and to society, Plato felt, could be solved only by developing an enlightened citizenry. All students, being potential citizens, must receive a common education. The general education was a liberal education. While all students received vocational training Plato held that education in the humanities enabled citizens to have the cultural support needed to make wise and good decisions.

The *Utopia* written by More followed the Platonic tradition which emphasized the intellect. Moral and intellectual freedom were rights all men should have, said More. The function of the schools was to produce citizens of cultural tastes and occupational efficiency. The state had the responsibility to mitigate poverty, waste and inefficiency. More believed, as Plato did, that education was the only means whereby men could secure the techniques that would make them free. The schools of Utopia were charged with the search for truth. More, in the utopian tradition, believed that only truth could promote freedom. Specifically More developed the following educational principles: (1) teachers should be of the highest moral and intellectual caliber, as befitted the guardians of the youth; (2) reading was the primary source of learning; and (3) true pleasure resulted from intellectual pursuits.

More summed up his educational philosophy in this manner: "The pleasures of the mind lie in knowledge, and in that delight which the contemplation of truth carries with it."[2]

Christianopolis was a reform writing which followed the utopian tradition, but with emphasis upon Christian principles. As the *Divine Comedy* was a visionary work steeped in Roman Catholic theology, and *Pilgrim's Progress* was representative of Puritanism, the *Christianopolis* was a work following the religious teachings of Luther. The schools in *Christianopolis,* said Andreae should teach Christian values, incorporating liberal and humanistic ideals. Andreae initiated a broad, comprehensive curriculum which included not only the liberal arts, but also the sciences and vocational education. Courses were taught with the idea that the end of man was to secure glory in the next world. Thus, Andreae differed with such materialists as Bacon. Andreae in the *Christianopolis* posited the following principles: (1) a system of educational psychology, based upon the idea of individual differences, and (2) that audio-visual materials and methods were among the most important tools of education.

Campanella, in the *City of the Sun,* followed the utopian tradition making freedom the greatest good and chief aim of man. The schools of the *City of the Sun* had the prime function of teaching man to be free. Freedom was not license; it was not undisciplined, said Campanella. Rather it was the right of free inquiry and deliberate choice. Training in the liberal arts helped one to make wise decisions. Campanella felt that occupational training enabled the citizen to attain economic security.

In the *City of the Sun* the following postulates were developed: (1) the curriculum included character education and vocational training; (2) learning took place primarily by means of the senses, thus audio-visual materials and methods were a vital part of the teacher's method; (3) pre-school training and adult education were an important function of the school system; and (4) education was compulsory and state supported.

Bacon held that the improvement of man's physical and social conditions was the highest requirement of morality and thus the duty of the state. The schools in the *New Atlantis* had the prime duty of developing citizens who could produce for themselves and the community the good things of life. Knowledge was the single most important thing in life, for it could produce new inventions and riches. The schools were the repository of knowledge. The schools could give man control over the forces of nature by teaching the sciences. Thus, the curriculum in the *New Atlantis* was essentially scientific. The educational principles contained in the *New Atlantis* included: (1) the purpose of education was to give a knowledge of natural laws; (2) colleges had the primary duty of research and publication; and (3) the coordinated activities of the college were aimed at the improvement of human life.

The *Social Contract* and *Emile,* the works of Rousseau, have had far-reaching effects upon modern education. The *Emile* focused pedagogical attention upon the child. Rousseau proposed several educational ideas. They were: (1) education should be child-centered; (2) education should be based upon psychological principles; (3) education should deal with real, life situations; (4) reading should be an essential part of education; (5) discipline should be taught, but it must be natural discipline; (6) female education should be related to adult roles; (7) vocational education should be part of the curriculum; and (8) education should aim at cultivating good taste.

Rousseau emphasized certain areas related to education. They were the sacredness of childhood, mild discipline, self-instruction, the value of simplicity, faith in God, and the belief that what is natural is good.

The utopists were quick to realize that the improvement of educational practices could not be actualized without changing all aspects of human social life. Thus, for example, the reform writers were among the first men to propose the abolition of drudgery and the dignifying of labor. They also believed in religious toleration. The idea of the short working day, reduced, for example, to four hours Campanella, was original with the utopists. These writers were among the most advanced social thinkers of their times, but it is virtually impossible for their schemes to be put into practice in their entirety. However, such concepts as the social theory of property, wherein the role of the state was envisaged as the prime agency in promoting cooperation among its citizens and promotion of the good of all, helped subsequent reformers actualize a state conducive to common good. The concept of the equality of the sexes is traceable to the utopists. Perhaps one of the most significant of the concepts produced by these reform writers was that of eugenics. The utopists believed in the perfectability of the human race, and they had tremendous faith in man's ability to surpass the limits of his biological nature; but they did not limit their hope to the use of the will alone. The movement of preventative medicine received, in part, impetus from each of the utopian writers. The idea of a medical school and a nursing school was incorporated in the works of Campanella and Bacon. Geriatrics was first proposed by Andreae. However, the most significant contribution made by these men was their idea that education was the most important institution within the state.

The philosophy of education of the utopists contained the ideal that all persons regardless of age, sex, or status had the right to education. The state had the duty to insure this right by issuing compulsory school attendance laws. Further, they felt that the state had a duty to see that the schools turned out the best possible citizens by educating the whole man; that is, the utopists believed that education must lead to the development of cultured citizens who possessed civic competence as well as a sound vocational orientation, a basis for successful family living, and an understanding of the techniques for health and physical fitness. The utopists held that the schools must encourage the students to develop habits of critical thinking. A critical method of inquiry (later referred to by Bacon as the scientific method) was deemed important because the utopists believed that the solutions to man's problems could be found in this world, indicating a strong tendency on the part of the utopists to rely as little as possible upon any theological orientation, and that the schools must teach the techniques to solve human problems.

The structure of the schools was first conceived by Plato and subsequently followed by the remaining utopists in the basic plan of an elementary school, secondary school, and college. The utopists believed that the secondary school should give vocational training to those students who would not go on to advanced studies, nor who displayed little interest in scholastic achievement. Those students who prepared for college work should receive, said the utopists, special studies of a college preparatory nature. The utopists also stated that each student should receive a general education so that all the students would have some similarity in educational background, and thus feel a sense of brotherhood with the whole community. Several different proposals were made regarding this general education. More, fore example, felt it should be based upon the classics. Other utopists such as Andreae and Campanella included basic vocational arts subjects in the area of general education. Since the utopists felt that education was the most important agency within the state it was axiomatic that they would take the control of the school out of the hands of private individuals and place the control under a governmental department. However, there existed a general feeling among the utopian writers that the direction of the schools should rest at least in part with the community. The reform writers stated that the needs of the community must be reflected in the curriculum.

Several contributions were made in the area of curriculum by the utopists. The whole program which is followed in the schools of science of the modern university was first conceived by Francis Bacon. He also advocated the study of what is now referred to as social psychology. Rousseau and Andreae promoted courses in political science. The systematic study of the homemaking arts was an original idea of the utopists, as were the courses in nursing arts and medical sciences. The systematized study of the physical arts was proposed by the utopists who felt that exercise not only was conducive to health, but promoted agility and grace.

Equality of educational opportunity for women was a utopian dream. The utopists were among the first to advocate equal opportunity for women in all activities and in particular in the area of education. Indeed the utopists were of the opinion that if a woman possessed the ability she should be considered for leading governmental positions. Rousseau was the only writer who placed a limit on the extent of female education. The remaining utopists stated in effect that women could attend school, even graduate school, as long as they profited by attendance.

Each utopist wrote explicit directions for the inclusion of courses in vocational education in his reform schemes of education. A few of the utopists, notably More, Andreae and Campanella, felt that all students, in order to promote a genuine feeling of democracy in the contact with all types of future workers, should take a basic course in agriculture and spend some time on the farms. These three utopists shared the feeling that this work in agriculture would encourage a love of nature. This system of agricultural apprenticeship supplied the state with a chief source of available labor. The utopists were adamant in the belief that all citizens should work. They were also concerned with the problem of granting increased dignity to labor. The utopists felt that if everybody worked, a four or six hour work day would be possible. The reform writers all agreed that the citizens of their future states should have a great deal of leisure time and that this leisure time should be spent in the main in educational pursuits.

A natural concomitant to increased leisure time was adult education. There is, for example, in the work of More and Campanella a suggestion that adult education be made compulsory. The utopists proposed a form of formal or informal adult education, including courses in the humanities as well as classes designed to increase occupational efficiency.

Character education was considered a vital aspect of the school. However, while some of the utopists, notably More, Andreae, and Campanella, proposed actual courses in character education, all agreed that the most important method of teaching moral and character development was by means of imitation. In particular they felt that the students should have teachers who were worthy of emulation. Contemporary society has lost sight of this utopian idea in that there is little premium paid or prestige attached to the teaching profession. More persons of high caliber would be attracted to teaching today if the rewards were greater.

The utopists emphasized the idea that all learning took place through the senses. Therefore, they stressed audio-visual materials and methods. Such adjuncts to teaching as museums, laboratories, zoos, parks, gardens and enclosures, libraries, murals and pictures were proposed by the utopists. Andreae proposed that the whole city be made into one vast educational edifice by painting educational murals on the walls.

The educational psychology of the utopists stated in effect that education must be adapted to the natural desires and wishes of the child. The utopists were concerned with discipline and considered it efficacious only if it was meted out in a fair manner and its purpose was understood by the child. Levels of understanding were considered when planning the curriculum. The reform writers believed that the course content of their schools must be on the level of the child's achievement. For example, play was considered as an educational tool in teaching the young; lessons for young children which were presented in an enjoyable manner were thought to be very effective by the utopists. In general the utopists felt that learning was not best under the lecture method. In the main, they felt that in using a continuum to display effective learning and teaching techniques, the lecture method would be at one end of a scale and the reading of the classics would fall at the superior end, with visual education utilizing pictures, laboratories, etc., as a close second in effective teaching techniques.

The contributions of the utopists have been an influence in the field of education. Their ideas have been in part actualized. Perhaps one of the most significant lessons contained in the spirit of utopianism, aside from the basic demand for excellence, is that the radical schemes of today's dreamers must not be discredited, for the possibility exists that their hopes and schemes may become part of the mainstream of future thought.

NOTES

Chapter One

1. Edward Bellamy, *Looking Backward* (New York: Ticknor and Co., 1888).
2. Aristotle, *The Politics* (Richard McKeon editor, New York: Random House, 1941), p. 1314.
3. Thucydides, *The Peloponnesian War* (Baltimore Md.: Penguin Classics, 1954), p. 118.
4. H. D. F. Kitto, *The Greeks* (Baltimore, Md.: Pelican Books, 1954), p. 136.
5. The Peloponnesian War virtually saw the end of the city-state as a creative force fashioning and fulfilling the lives of all its members. During the fourth century Greece steadily moved toward new ways of thought and a new way of life; so much so that to those who were born at the end of this century, the age of Pericles must have seemed as remote, mentally, as the Middle Ages do to us. Kitto, *ibid.*, p. 152.
6. William Ebenstein, *Great Political Thinkers* (New York: Rinehart and Co., 1954), p. 168.
7. See Harry W. Laidler, *Social Economic Movements* (New York: Thomas Y. Crowell Co., 1948), and also Edmund Wilson, *To The Finland Station* (Garden City: Doubleday & Co., 1953).
8. Henry Steel Commager, *Living Ideas in America* (New York: Harper Bros., Inc.).
9. Karl Marx and Friedrich Engels, *The Communist Manifesto,* in William Ebenstein, *Great Political Thinkers* (Princeton: Rinehart and Co., 1954), p. 669.

Chapter Two

1. Bertrand Russell, *A History of Western Philosophy* (New York: Simon and Schuster, 1954), p. 104.
2. "Plato son of Ariston and Perictine, was born in 428/7 B.C. and died at the age of eighty or eighty-one, in 148/7. Both parents came from distinguished families." Francis MacDonald Cornford, *The Republic of Plato* (New York: Oxford University Press), p. xv.
3. A. E. Taylor, *Plato, The Man and His Work* (London: Methuen & Company, 1949), p. 3.
4. A. E. Taylor, *ibid.*, p. 5.
5. Plato discusses this in the *Republic* and uses the anthropomorphizing of the gods as a basis for the rejection of Homer and Hesiod in his schools.
6. "Social justice (in the *Republic*) may be defined as the principle of a society, consisting of different types of men who have combined under the impulse of their need for one another, and by their combination in one

society, and their concentration on their separate functions, have made a whole which is perfect because it is the product and the image of the whole of the human mind."

Ernest Barker, *Greek Political Theory, Plato and His Predecessors* (New York: Henry Holt and Co., 1925), p. 176.

7. Plato, *op. cit.*, p. 127.
8. Plato, *op. cit.*, p. 132.
9. Plato, *op. cit.*, p. 132.
10. Plato, *op. cit.*, p. 121.
11. Plato describes the variations in learning, that is between the level of knowledge and of opinion in this manner:

> Here is a parable to illustrate the degrees in which our nature may be enlightened or unenlightened. Imagine the condition of men living in a sort of cavernous chamber underground, with an entrance open to the light and a long passage all down the cave. Here they have been from childhood, chained by the leg and also by the neck, so that they cannot move, and can see only what is in front of them, because the chains will not let them turn their heads. At some distance higher up is the light of a fire burning behind them; and between the prisoners and the fire is a track with a parapet built along it like the screen at a puppet show, which hides the performers while they show their puppets over the top. Now behind this parapet imagine persons carrying along various artificial objects, including figures of men and animals in wood, or stone, or other materials. The prisoners so confined would see nothing except the shadows thrown by the fire-light on the wall. Suppose one of them were set free, and, when he had come out into the light, find his eyes so full of its radiance that he could not see a single one of the things he was told were real? He would need to grow accustomed to images and things themselves. Now imagine what would happen if he went down again to take his former seat in the Cave. Coming suddenly out of the sunlight, his eyes would be filled with darkness. If he delivers opinions again on the shadows the other prisoners will laugh at him and say that he had gone up only to come back with his sight ruined.

12. Plato, *op. cit.*, p. 231.
13. Grube says: "Great importance is attached in the *Republic* to order and harmony in the soul. This is necessary, not only to the philosopher for whom all virtues are truly one since they all inevitably follow from his wisdom and knowledge of Forms, but even the lowest class must possess sophrosyne (sic) and justice."

G. M. A. Grube, *Plato's Thought* (London: Methuen and Co. Ltd., 1935), p. 226.

14. Plato said: "It will be the business of reason to rule with wisdom and fore-thought on behalf of the entire soul." *op. cit.*, p. 140.
15. Plato, *op. cit.*, p. 215.
16. Plato, *op. cit.*, p. 215.
17. St. Augustine states of Plato: "He saw that the causes of things were sought for by them—which causes he believed to be ultimately reducible to nothing else than the will of the true and supreme God." St. Augustine, *The City of God* (New York: Modern Library, 1950), p. 246.
18. Plato, *op. cit.*, p. 73.

19. Plato, *op. cit.*, p. 220.
20. Plato, *op. cit.*, p. 676.
21. Plato, *op. cit.*, p. 246.
22. Plato, *op. cit.*, p. 246.
23. Plato, *op. cit.*, p. 115.
24. Aristophanes wrote a play based upon this concept of Plato's entitled "The Ecclesiazusae." Eugene O'Neill, Jr. called this play a utopia stating that in it the women ". . . seized power, and established a community of property as a panacea for all the social and economic ills which beset Athens in the first two decades of the fourth century."

Eugene O'Neill, Jr., *"The Complete Greek Drama"* (New York: Random House, 1938), p. 1003.

25. Plato, *op. cit.*, p. 717.
26. Plato, *op. cit.*, p. 232.
27. Plato, *op. cit.*, p. 258.
28. Plato devoted almost exclusively the section on elementary education to literature and music.
29. Plato, *op. cit.*, p. 69.
30. Plato, *op. cit.*, p. 74.
31. Plato, *op. cit.*, p. 83.
32. Plato, *op. cit.*, p. 89.
33. Plato, *op. cit.*, p. 241.
34. Plato, *op. cit.*, p. 242.
35. Plato, *op. cit.*, p. 244.
36. Plato, *op. cit.*, p. 244.
37. Plato, *op. cit.*, p. 250.
38. In the analogy of the cave the study of mathematics might be compared to the period when the prisoner is leaving the cave and sees, for the first time, real objects; however, the objects will still appear in shadow due to the fact that the prisoner's eyes have not become completely accustomed to the light. The period of dialectic is comparable to the time when, after the prisoner's eyes are accustomed to the light, he sees things as they really are.
39. Plato, *op. cit.*, p. 252.
40. Plato, *op. cit.*, p. 255.
41. Plato, *op. cit.*, p. 78.
42. Plato, *op. cit.*, p. 78.
43. Plato, *op. cit.*, p. 124.
44. Plato, *op. cit.*, p. 126.
45. Plato, *op. cit.*, p. 90.
46. Plato, *op. cit.*, p. 83.
47. Plato, *op. cit.*, p. 215.
48. Plato, *op. cit.*, p. 667.
49. Plato, *op. cit.*, p. 696.
50. Plato discussed this problem in the following quotation:

> Why we valiantly and pugnaciously insist, that different natures ought to have different pursuits, but we never considered at all what was the meaning of sameness or difference of nature, or why we distinguished them when we assigned different pursuits to different natures

> and the same natures . . . Man and women alike possess the qualities which make a guardian; they differ only in their comparative strength or weakness . . . You will admit that the same education which makes a man a good guardian will make a woman a good guardian; for their original nature is the same.
> Plato, *op. cit.*, p. 714.

51. Plato, *op. cit.*, p. 796.
52. Plato, *op. cit.*, p. 68.
53. The three levels of the soul compared to the three occupational levels. Plato contended that by the very nature of their soul men could be placed in a certain political or occupational group. These three levels are distinct groupings allowing for no shading or blurring of the edges between them.
54. Plato, *op. cit.*, p. 131.
55. Plato, *op. cit.*, p. 89.
56. Plato, *op. cit.*, p. 124.
57. Plato, *op. cit.*, p. 138.
58. Plato, *op. cit.*, p. 715.
59. Arthur Henry Hoehlman and Joseph S. Roucek, *Comparative Education* (New York: Dryden Press, 1951), p. 9ff.

Chapter Three

1. Karl Kautsky, *Thomas More and His Utopia* (New York: Russell and Russell, 1948), p. 14ff.
2. E. E. Reynolds, *Thomas More* (New York: Doubleday and Co., 1958), p. 15.
3. At the same time More was writing the *Utopia* Luther wrote his 95 Thesis, and Machiavelli wrote the *Prince*.
4. Thomas More, *Utopia* (London: J. M. Dent and Sons Ltd., 1951), p. 23.
5. More, *ibid.*, p. 28.
6. More was opposed to the type of pleasure pursued by the wealthy class because he considered it mere concupiscence. In the *Utopia* he repeatedly praised the right type of pleasure—which for him meant good health, a right conscience, and the joy derived from learning.
7. More intended the list of commodities to include not only food, drink, clothing, and shelter, but also work, leisure, and education.
8. Exchange with foreign countries was carried on by means of barter.
9. More said in an optimistic but naive statement:

> The young and the old sit together in the dining halls, the reason is that the gravity of the old people, and the reverence due them, might restrain the younger from all indecent words and gestures.
> More, *op. cit.*, p. 106.

10. More wanted to be sure that his proposed society could be controlled in times of stress by a few men who had vitually absolute power. These men could at other times rig the social conditions to achieve certain ends.

11. Perhaps More felt that the *Utopia* would indicate to his contemporaries that his ideal state was subject to change, because it could be surpassed by divine revelation.

12. More considered learning as being the greatest pleasure and it might be advantageous to see what he meant by pleasure. He wrote the *Utopia* in Latin because the scholarly writing of his time was done in that language. He used the term "voluptas" which has appeared in all translations as "pleasure." In Latin the word "voluptas" has two meanings: the first signifies physical or sense enjoyment, and the second mental enjoyment. More also used the term to convey the idea of religious joy in contemplating God's handiworks. See in particular p. 84 to p. 94.

13. "Happiness does not rest in all pleasure, but only in that pleasure that is good and honest." More, *op. cit.*, p. 84.

14. More, *op. cit.*, p. 84.

15. More, *op. cit.*, p. 87.

16. More, *op. cit.*, p. 88.

17. More, *op. cit.*, p. 72.

18. More, *op. cit.*, p. 61.

19. More, *op. cit.*, p. 85.

20. More, *op. cit.*, p. 85ff.

21. More, *op. cit.*, p. 85.

22. In order to provide ample time for learning, the citizens' manual labor was reduced to a minimum of six hours a day.

23. More, *op. cit.*, p. 92.

24. More, *op. cit.*, p. 83.

25. More, *op. cit.*, p. 83.

26. The small logicals were very important in history of logic, philosophy and education in Western Europe. The men who did the most to develop the small logicals were Duns Scotus and William of Ockham. The universities of Paris, Cologne, Vienna, Freiburg, Leipzig, Ingolsadt, and Tübingen used the works of Duns Scotus and Ockham as a text.

Bertrand Russell, *A History of Western Philosophy* (New York: Simon and Schuster, 1945), p. 388; and Will Durant, *The Age of Faith* (New York; Simon and Schuster, 1950), p. 913ff.

27. Discontent with the subtlety of the Scholastics had been in evidence for several centuries; notable among the critics were John of Salisbury and Peter of Blois. See Durant, *ibid.*, p. 958.

28. More, *op. cit.*, p. 69.

29. More, *op. cit.*, p. 82.

30. More, *op. cit.*, p. 67.

31. More, *op. cit.*, p. 82.

32. The general humanistic program of Erasmus and Colet for intellectual and education reform which influenced More also demanded the elimination of the practices and works of the scholastics and a return to the "Great Books."

33. Etienne Gilson, *The Spirit of Medieval Philosophy* (New York: Charles Scribner's Sons, 1940), p. 403.

34. See in particular Richard McKeon's introduction to the *Works of*

Aristotle (New York: Random House, 1941), p. vii, and Russell, *op. cit.*, p. 101.

35. More, *op. cit.*, p. 94.

36. The demand for a return to the original and primary works has already been seen in More's dislike for the innumerable commentaries of the Scholastics. The fact that More did include Aristotle in his list of books was also meant to be a strong suggestion to the Scholastics to rid themselves of the useless and needlessly complex commentaries and return to the original treatises of Aristotle. The Scholastics could then earn their title of Aristotelians by studying all the works of their deified Aristotle in Greek.

37. More, *op. cit.*, p. 95.

38. More, *op. cit.*, p. 83.

39. More, *op. cit.*, p. 83.

40. More, *op. cit.*, p. 84.

41. More, *op. cit.*, p. 125.

42. More, *op. cit.*, p. 78.

43. More, *op. cit.*, p. 79.

44. More, *op. cit.*, p. 125.

45. More, *op. cit.*, p. 114.

46. More, *op. cit.*, p. 83.

47. More, *op. cit.*, p. 85.

48. More, *op. cit.*, p. 85.

49. More, *op. cit.*, p. 85.

50. More, *op. cit.*, p. 103.

51. More, *op. cit.*, p. 74.

52. More, *op. cit.*, p. 69.

53. Campanella called his school system the very center of the state, and Bacon referred to his school as the eye of the kingdom.

54. More, *op. cit.*, p. 74.

55. More, *op. cit.*, p. 74.

56. More, *op. cit.*, p. 65.

57. The economy of Utopia was based upon agriculture. Farm products were the only commodity exported to other nations.

58. More, *op. cit.*, p. 58.

59. More, *op. cit.*, p. 58.

60. More, *op. cit.*, p. 61.

61. The Utopia contained several inconsistencies, as has already been pointed out. One major inconsistency was More's statement that learning was the Utopian's chief pleasure and that the gardens were his chief source of pleasure. More, *op. cit.*, p. 61.

62. More, *op. cit.*, p. 61.

63. Arthur Henry Moehlman and Joseph S. Roucek, *Comparative Education* (New York: Dryden Press, 1951), p. 2.

64. H. G. Good, *A History of Western Education* (New York: Macmillan Company, 1953), p. 496.

65. Good, *ibid.*, p. 450.

66. Moehlman and Roucek, *op. cit.*, p. 29.

67. Moehlman and Roucek, *op. cit.*, p. 166.
68. Moehlman and Roucek, *op. cit.*, p. 171.
69. Moehlman and Roucek, *op. cit.*, p. 320.
70. Moehlman and Roucek, *op. cit.*, p. 247.
71. Moehlman and Roucek, *op. cit.*, p. 6.
72. Among the minor ideas which have not been accepted and which because they possess little merit will probably never be accepted except perhaps on a small scale are: (1) dormitories for all schools, (2) state nursery care for the very young child, (3) teachers who function also as religious leaders, (4) Greek classics as basic text in all colleges, (5) compulsory basic vocational education course in agriculture, (6) uniform dress for all students, (7) courses in logic in elementary and secondary schools, (8) science courses based upon classical Greek concept and method, (9) common meals for all students with moral and cultural readings.
73. Persons granted a loan by the Department of Health, Welfare, and Education for the purpose of teacher training may have the debt cancelled at the rate of 1/5 of the total amount every year they remain in teaching. If they continue in teaching for five years half of the debt is automatically cancelled. *National Defense Education Act of 1958, A Summary of the Committee on Labor and Public Welfare United States Senate, September 5, 1958* (Washington, D.C.: United States Government Printing Office, 1958), p. 1.
74. The only exception was vocational education.

Chapter Four

1. Campanella grounded his religious concepts upon the theological ideas expressed by Plato and More. Campanella's ideas included: (1) the rejection of supernatural revelations, (2) the idea that God can be made known through the act of reasoning, and (3) the embodiment of naturalistic-ascetic principles of goodness.
2. The only work which has been translated from the Italian into English and published in this country is the *City of the Sun*. The *City of the Sun* was first translated by Morely at the beginning of the century. The translation was unsatisfactory in many respects. The second translation was done by William J. Gilstrop and is included in Glenn Negley's and J. M. Patrick's *The Quest for Utopia* (New York: Henry Schuman, 1952), p. 43. The only book published in English which deals exclusively with Campanella is Francisco Grillo, *Tommaso Campanella in America* (New York: S. F. Vanne Co., 1954).
3. "Private property owes its origin and development to each individual's having his own house, wife, and children. From this arises selfishness; for in order to raise a son to riches and honors and leave him as heir to much wealth, each of us becomes either desirous of seizing control of the state or greedy, contriving, and hypocritical. But when men have rid themselves of selfishness, there remains only love for the community." Campanella, *ibid.*, p. 322.

4. Campanella felt that love was a psychological drive and that if its object, property, was removed the drive would attempt to secure its object in the whole community.

5. Campanella, *op. cit.*, p. 323.

6. "The citizens of the City of the Sun determined to lead a philosophic life in common. The community of wives is the custom among them. All things are held in common, so that no one can appropriate anything for himself."

7. Campanella, *op. cit.*, p. 333.

8. Campanella, *op. cit.*, p. 336.

9. Campanella, *op. cit.*, p. 331.

10. For example, Campanella defended his position regarding marriage in this manner: "This function of breeding humans has reference to the state and not to individuals, except in so far as they are members of the state. And since individuals generally bring forth children wrongly and rear them wrongly, to the great detriment of the state, this function is scrupulously committed to the magistrates as the main basis of the state." Campanella, *op. cit.*, p. 322.

11. Campanella, *op. cit.*, p. 327.

12. Campanella, *op. cit.*, p. 327.

13. Campanella, *op. cit.*, p. 333.

14. Only teachers were considered for promotion to the highest ranks. Campanella, *op. cit.*, p. 340.

15. An interesting aspect of the healthful conditions of the citizens is the fact that they did not have to endanger their health by taking long and arduous trips on foot or horseback. The inhabitants of this utopia which was proposed in the sixteenth century had the choice of two modes of transportation. They could fly, for ". . . they have already discovered the art of flying," "or they could ride in cars propelled by the wind," as, "They use wagons fitted with sails which are borne along even by a contrary wind through a skillful arrangement of wheels against wheels." Campanella, *op. cit.*, p. 335, 346.

16. Campanella, *op. cit.*, p. 328.

17. Campanella, *op. cit.*, p. 345.

18. Campanella, *op. cit.*, p. 338.

19. Campanella, *op. cit.*, p. 338.

20. Campanella, *op. cit.*, p. 338.

21. Campanella, *op. cit.*, p. 338.

22. Campanella, *op. cit.*, p. 338.

23. Campanella, *op. cit.*, p. 338.

24. The inconsistencies, ambiguities, and lack of perception in regards to human nature in the political philosophy have induced exponents of divergent political opinions to accept Campanella as an early advocate of their system. The utopian writers evidently considered human nature more honorable than other authors considering human nature.

25. This figure was copied after the political and religious role of the Pope. Campanella, *op. cit.*, p. 320.

26. Campanella, *op. cit.*, p. 322.

27. Campanella, *op. cit.*, p. 333.

28. Campanella was committed to the proposition that science possessed techniques necessary for and applicable to the improvement of society. Science had a two-fold interest for Campanella. Science enabled men to exploit nature; it also supplied the means to construct and engineer a society that would supply the whole population with the material and spiritual means to make life, if not idyllic at least content and secure.

29. Campanella, *op. cit.*, p. 328.

30. Campanella, *op. cit.*, p. 327.

31. Campanella, *op. cit.*, p. 324.

32. Astrology, cosmology, geometry, history, poetry, logic, rhetoric, grammar, medicine, physics, politics, and ethics. Campanella, *op. cit.*, p. 320.

33. Campanella, *op. cit.*, p. 326.

34. Campanella, *op. cit.*, p. 327.

35. Campanella, *op. cit.*, p. 321.

36. Campanella, *op. cit.*, p. 324.

37. Campanella said, "Men and women alike follow the mechanical and the theoretical occupations, with this difference, that the occupations which require more hard work and those in which one has to go some distance are practiced by men." Campanella, *op. cit.*, p. 327.

38. "If a woman does not conceive with one man she is mated with others, and if at length she is found to be barren, she is made available for communal use, but she is not given the honorable standing of married women in the Council of Procreation in the temple." Campanella, *op. cit.*, p. 330.

39. The reform writers made a point of developing their ideas extensively in the area of religion also. Rousseau inserted what appeared to be a complete essay on his religious beliefs, "The Creed of a Savoyard Priest," in the *Emile*. Plato developed original and penetrating ideas related in part to religion in the *Republic*, and the *Timeaus*, has had profound effects upon Christian theology. Andreae's *Christianopolis* was primarily a religious state devoted to producing highly moral citizens. In the *New Atlantis* as well as in More's *Utopia* there was the development of theological systems and provisions for furthering the moral development of the people by means of character education and religious sanctions.

40. Campanella, *op. cit.*, p. 343.

41. Campanella, *op. cit.*, p. 344.

42. This concept further developed by Rousseau ultimately influenced Kant resulting in the categorical imperative. See Ernst Cassirer, *Rousseau, Kant, Goethe* (Princeton: Princeton University Press, 1947), p. 55.

43. Campanella, *op. cit.*, p. 334.

44. Campanella, *op. cit.*, p. 323.

45. Campanella, *op. cit.*, p. 340.

46. For example, a man or woman who remained a virgin until the age of twenty-seven received special awards. This is inconsistent with Campanella's position that procreation was a basic need for the survival of the state.

47. Campanella, *op. cit.*, p. 322.

48. Campanella, *op. cit.*, p. 340.

49. Campanella, *op. cit.*, p. 323.
50. Campanella (and More) required that all citizens of the new state take the basic course in agriculture.
51. Campanella, *op. cit.*, p. 324.
52. Campanella, *op. cit.*, p. 334.
53. Campanella, *op. cit.*, p. 336.
54. Campanella, *op. cit.*, p. 334.
55. Among the chief goals that Campanella felt would be attained was the inculcation of the love of learning.
56. Campanella, *op. cit.*, p. 286.
57. Campanella, *op. cit.*, p. 280.
58. Many of the ideas expounded by Campanella were also held by his utopian predecessors, thus such ideas that have been actualized were discussed in chapters III and IV.
59. See Charles F. Schuller, *The School Administrator and His Audio-Visual Program* (Washington, D.C.: Department of Audio-Visual Instruction, National Education Association, 1954); W. A. Wittich, and John G. Fowlkes, *Audio-Visual Paths to Learning* (New York: Harper and Bros., 1945); Varney C. Arnspiger, *Measuring the Effectiveness of Sound Motion Pictures as Teaching Aids* (New York: Columbia University, 1933); *Audio-Visual Materials of Instruction,* Forty-Eighth Yearbook, Part I (Chicago: U. of Chicago Press, 1949); Ben Wood and Frank Freeman, *Motion Pictures in the Classroom* (New York: Houghton Mifflin Co., 1929).
60. Harry W. Laidler, *Social-Economic Movements* (New York: Crowell Company, 1948), p. 36.
61. Moehlman and Roucek, *op. cit.*, p. 166ff.
62. Moehlman and Roucek, *op. cit.*, p. 371ff.
63. Moehlman and Roucek, *op. cit.*, p. 157ff.
64. Several of Campanella's ideas not realized as yet appear, because they have little value, never to be actualized. They include the idea that all students should live in dormitories attached to the schools, instruction in the alphabet before the age of three, and intense concentration in a survey course that would last from the age of three to seven, during which time the student was expected to make an intelligent and critical choice concerning his future occupation. The use of dormitories is not feasible from an economic standpoint as well as the fact that it would have detrimental effects upon the family structure. Psychological studies (See, for example, Arnold Gesell and Francis Illg, *The Child From One To Five,* chapter one, and *The Child From Five To Ten* [New York: Harper and Bros., 1946], p. 13) have indicated that children in the main, cannot be expected profitably to engage in reading before the age of six and one-half. To expect a child of seven or less to make intelligent choices regarding occupational choice is manifestly naive.
65. James B. Conant, *The American High School Today* (New York: McGraw Hill Book Co., Inc., 1959).
66. Conant, *ibid.*, p. 73.
67. Conant, *ibid.*, p. 47.
68. Good stated, "The *City of the Sun* was opposed to narrow specializa-

tion and favored instead an encyclopedic and more general knowledge and training." Good, *op. cit.*, p. 174.

69. *Current History*, Vol. 35, No. 204 (June, 1958).

70. Jacques Barzun, *The Teacher in America* (Garden City: Doubleday and Co., 1954); and Thorstein Veblen, *The Higher Learning in America* (New York: Sagmore Press Inc., 1957).

71. Conant, *op. cit.*, p. 50.

72. Conant, *op. cit.*, p. 67.

73. Laidler, *op. cit.*, p. 37.

74. Found at least in the western world.

Chapter Five

1. Felix Emil Held, *Christianopolis, An Ideal State Of The Seventeenth Century* (New York: Oxford University Press, 1916), p. 10.

2. Alfred North Whitehead, *Science and the Modern World* (New York: The New American Library Co., 1958), p. 39.

3. Only the *Christianopolis* has been translated into English and published in this country.

4. Johann Valentin Andreae, *Christianopolis* (New York: Oxford University Press, 1916), p. 135.

5. Andreae, *op. cit.*, p. 258.

6. Andreae, *op. cit.*, p. 261.

7. Andreae, *op. cit.*, p. 263.

8. Andreae, *op. cit.*, p. 274.

9. Andreae, *op. cit.*, p. 274.

10. Andreae stated in his book that the hero of the church in Christianopolis was Doctor Luther. Andreae, *op. cit.*, p. 234.

11. Andreae, *op. cit.*, p. 159.

12. Andreae, *op. cit.*, p. 177.

13. Andreae, *op. cit.*, p. 159.

14. Andreae, *op. cit.*, p. 237.

15. Andreae, *op. cit.*, p. 174.

16. Andreae, *op. cit.*, p. 174.

17. Andreae, *op. cit.*, p. 174.

18. A superior person was defined by Andreae as one who was God-fearing, pious, moral and a devotee of science and the humanities, see Andreae, *op. cit.*, p. 148.

19. Andreae, *op. cit.*, p. 173.

20. Andreae included a map with the edition of his book showing this pattern.

21. Andreae, *op. cit.*, p. 173.

22. Andreae, *op. cit.*, p. 154.

23. Andreae, *op. cit.*, p. 154.

24. Andreae and Rousseau were the only utopists who admitted to change in their writings.

25. Andreae, *op. cit.*, p. 186.

26. Andreae, *op. cit.*, p. 166.

27. Andreae, *op. cit.*, p. 209.

28. Andreae, *op. cit.*, p. 208.
29. Andreae, *op. cit.*, p. 205.
30. Andreae, *op. cit.*, p. 206.
31. Andreae, *op. cit.*, p. 206.
32. Andreae, *op. cit.*, p. 206.
33. Andreae, *op. cit.*, p. 207.
34. Andreae, *op. cit.*, p. 207.
35. Andreae, *op. cit.*, p. 210.
36. Andreae, *op. cit.*, p. 198.
37. Andreae, *op. cit.*, p. 198.
38. Andreae, *op. cit.*, p. 210.
39. Andreae, *op. cit.*, p. 211.
40. Andreae, *op. cit.*, p. 214.
41. Andreae, *op. cit.*, p. 213.
42. Andreae, *op. cit.*, p. 212.
43. Andreae, *op. cit.*, p. 213.
44. Andreae, *op. cit.*, p. 215.
45. Andreae, *op. cit.*, p. 216.
46. Andreae, *op. cit.*, p. 219.
47. Andreae, *op. cit.*, p. 219.
48. Andreae, *op. cit.*, p. 225.
49. Andreae, *op. cit.*, p. 231.
50. Andreae, *op. cit.*, p. 231.
51. Andreae, *op. cit.*, p. 232.
52. Andreae, *op. cit.*, p. 232.
53. Andreae, *op. cit.*, p. 236.
54. Andreae, *op. cit.*, p. 236.
55. Andreae, *op. cit.*, p. 216.
56. Andreae, *op. cit.*, p. 240.
57. Andreae, *op. cit.*, p. 240.
58. Andreae, *op. cit.*, p. 241.
59. Andreae used the term "political science" in his book and gave it essentially the same meaning that it has today. See Andreae, *op. cit.*, p. 238.
60. Andreae, *op. cit.*, p. 166.
61. Andreae, *op. cit.*, p. 198.
62. Andreae, *op. cit.*, p. 248.
63. Andreae, *op. cit.*, p. 246.
64. Andreae, *op. cit.*, p. 211.
65. Andreae, *op. cit.*, p. 125.
66. Andreae, *op. cit.*, p. 65.
67. Andreae spent a great deal of time discussing widowhood because remarriage was virtually forbidden in the *Christianopolis*.
68. Andreae, *op. cit.*, p. 263.
69. Andreae, *op. cit.*, p. 261.
70. Andreae, *op. cit.*, p. 242.
71. Andreae, *op. cit.*, p. 258.
72. Andreae, *op. cit.*, p. 258.
73. Andreae, *op. cit.*, p. 140.

74. Andreae, *op. cit.*, p. 163.
75. The moral quality of the community idealized in the *Christianopolis* undoubtedly influenced its counterparts which were actualized in the nineteenth century, in particular Brook Farm, New Harmony, the Oneida Colony and Nauvoo.
76. Andreae, *op. cit.*, p. 175.
77. Andreae, *op. cit.*, p. 164.
78. Andreae, *op. cit.*, p. 165.
79. Andreae, *op. cit.*, p. 256.
80. Andreae said, "It is far easier to tear out the first elements and roots of vice than to lop off the nature stalks." Andreae, *op. cit.*, p. 165.
81. Andreae, *op. cit.*, p. 163.
82. Andreae, *op. cit.*, p. 157.
83. Andreae, *op. cit.*, p. 161.
84. Andreae, *op. cit.*, p. 157.
85. Andreae, *op. cit.*, p. 157.
86. Andreae, *op. cit.*, p. 250.
87. Andreae, *op. cit.*, p. 168.
88. Andreae, *op. cit.*, p. 157.
89. Andreae, *op. cit.*, p. 157.
90. Andreae, *op. cit.*, p. 157.
91. Andreae, *op. cit.*, p. 193.
92. Andreae followed Luther in believing that each citizen should have his own copy of the Bible. Thus, one of the chief duties of the printing office was the publishing of the Bible.
93. Andreae, *op. cit.*, p. 196.
94. Andreae, *op. cit.*, p. 199.
95. Andreae, *op. cit.*, p. 204.
96. Andreae, *op. cit.*, p. 200.
97. See Gordon W. Allport, *Personality, A Psychological Interpretation* (New York: Henry Holt and Co., 1945), p. 151.
98. This included training in their subject field as well as in the areas of methods, educational philosophy and psychology.
99. See Held, *op. cit.*, p. 101.
100. Ideas proposed by Andreae and which will probably never be incorporated in educational practice include dormitory life for all students, the idea that teachers must marry teachers, apologetics as a required course in college, and teachers also being governmental functionaries.
101. Wendell Johnson, *People in Quandaries, The Semantics of Personal Adjustment* (New York and London: Harper Brothers, 1946), p. 243.

Chapter Six

1. For example, the schools were constantly determining means to improve health, transportation and diet, etc.
2. Francis Bacon, *New Atlantis* (New York: Walter J. Black Co., 1942), p. 258.
3. Bacon, *ibid.*, p. 288.
4. Bacon, *ibid.*, p. 272.

5. Though Bacon removed the search for final cause as a problem in philosophy he was not attempting to erect a system that was irreligious. He felt that religion was the basis for any well-ordered society. He was not anti-religious but was concerned with the removal of superstition from religion. For example, he said, "Miracles and wonders shall cease by reason that you shall discover their natural causes." Bacon, *ibid.*, p. 245.

6. The *New Atlantis* was similar to the *Christianopolis* in terms of the social pattern. The family was the primary unit; the state being erected upon this unit. The family pattern was essentially authoritarian. The oldest living male was the head of the family and this rank was not merely titular. In order to stabilize the family pattern the state utilized celebration; each male who had thirty living descendants was lauded at the "Feast of the Family." The purpose of the ceremony was to instill patriotism and civil as well as familial obedience. The feast was essentially religious, but the state intervened by financing the celebration. The king provided the father with a gold emblem which accorded him privileges. The state encouraged family unity and large families by means of this festival. Bacon, *ibid.*, p. 274.

7. One example of an impractical laboratory was a tower one-half mile high with which to study winds and atmospheric pressure. Bacon, *ibid.*, p. 289.

8. "There is no doubt that Bacon's project for Solomon's House in the *New Atlantis* was directly responsible for the constitution of the Royal Society in London." Lewis Mumford, *The Condition of Man* (New York: Harcourt, Brace and Co., 1944), p. 245.

9. Alfred North Whitehead, *Science in the Modern World* (New York: New American Library of World Literature, Inc., 1958), p. 44.

10. Bertrand Russell stated: "The whole basis of Bacon's philosophy was practical: to give mankind mastery over the forces of nature by means of scientific discoveries and inventions. He held that philosophy should be kept separate from theology, not intimately blended with it as in scholasticism. He accepted orthodox religion; he was not the man to quarrel with the government of such matter. But he thought that reason could show the existence of God, he regarded everything else in theology as known only by revelation." Bertrand Russell, *A History of Western Philosophy* (New York: Simon & Schuster, 1945), p. 542.

11. John Dewey, *Democracy and Education* (New York: Macmillan & Co., 1916), p. 342.

12. John Dewey, *Reconstruction in Philosophy* (Boston: Beacon Press, 1948), p. 38.

13. Basil Willey, *The Seventeenth Century Background* (New York: Doubleday Anchor Books, 1955), p. 32ff.

Chapter Seven

1. Jean Jacques Rousseau, *Social Contract* (New York: Tudor Publishing Co., 1940), p. 4.

2. Rousseau, *ibid.*, p. 24.

3. Jean Jacques Rousseau, *Emile* (New York: E. P. Dutton and Co., 1950), p. 5.

4. "The crisis is approaching, and we are on the edge of a revolution." Rousseau, *ibid.*, p. 157.

5. "I am never weary of repeating," said Rousseau, "let all the lessons of young people take the form of doing rather than talking, let them learn nothing from books which they can learn from experience." Rousseau, *op. cit.*, p. 214.

6. Rousseau, *op. cit.*, p. 19.

7. Rousseau, *op. cit.*, p. 59.

8. Rousseau, *op. cit.*, p. 84.

9. Rousseau, *op. cit.*, p. 305.

10. Rousseau, *op. cit.*, p. 305.

11. Rousseau, *op. cit.*, p. 305.

12. Rousseau, *op. cit.*, p. 306.

13. Rousseau, *op. cit.*, p. 306.

14. Rousseau attempted to do in the *Emile* what Plato did in the *Republic*; he proposed to study the macrocosm by means of the microcosm. He said:

> I have decided to take an imaginary pupil to assume on my part the age, health, knowledge, and talents required for the work of his education, to guide him from birth to manhood.
> Rousseau, *op. cit.*, p. 19.

Several authors have attempted to justify Rousseau's erecting the conditions surrounding *Emile*, which included a permanent tutor, the absence of parents, etc., as merely a device to facilitate the demonstration of his principles. It is impossible to justify Rousseau's position, because it is completely unrealistic; it was fundamentally anomalous, in that it proposed to erect a system of education whereby a teacher spent at least twenty-five years with one student, where only wealthy and healthy students could participate, and where the teacher practiced deceit utilizing highly structured learning situations, and culminated in the teacher's selection of his pupil's bride. These factors would result in an educational system that would not be universal or progressive and which would be forced to depend upon too much isolation. (See in particular: Matthew Josephson, *Jean-Jacques Rousseau* [New York: Harcourt Brace and Co., 1932], p. 18ff; F. C. Green, *Jean-Jacques Rousseau, A Critical Study of His Life and Writings* [Cambridge: Cambridge University Press, 1955], p. 226; and Robert R. Rusk, *The Doctrine of the Great Educators* [London: Macmillan and Co., Ltd., 1926], p. 143ff.)

15. Rousseau, *op. cit.*, p. 308.

16. Principally by William Henry Hudson, *Rousseau and Naturalism in Life and Thought* (Endinburgh: T. Clark Co., 1903), p. 183ff.

Thomas Davidson, *Rousseau and Education According To Nature* (New York: Charles Scribner and Sons, 1898), and John W. Chapman, *Rousseau—Totalitarian or Liberal* (New York: Columbia University Press, 1956), p. 142ff.

17. From this statement it is possible to assume that Rousseau would

have included in the list the works of Plato, Aristotle, Aristophanes. Rousseau specifically named the following: Xenophon, Cicero, Pliny, Thucydides, Herodotus, Commentaries of Caesar, Plutarch, to be part of the list of classical authors he proposed.

18. Rousseau, *op. cit.*, p. 309.
19. Rousseau, *op. cit.*, p. 311.
20. Rousseau gave profuse examples of good taste in the following areas: food and dining, clothing and attire, travel, home furnishing, and friendship. Rousseau, *op. cit.*, p. 311ff.
21. Rousseau, *op. cit.*, p. 316.
22. Rousseau, *op. cit.*, p. 13.
23. Rousseau, *op. cit.*, p. 15.
24. Rousseau, *op. cit.*, p. 8ff.
25. "By slow and careful stages children can learn to fear nothing." Rousseau, *op. cit.*, p. 31.
26. Rousseau, *op. cit.*, p. 33.
27. Rousseau, *op. cit.*, p. 35.
28. Rousseau, *op. cit.*, p. 57.
29. Rousseau, *op. cit.*, p. 54.
30. Rousseau, *op. cit.*, p. 59.
31. Rousseau, *op. cit.*, p. 51.
32. Rousseau, *op. cit.*, p. 52.
33. Rousseau, *op. cit.*, p. 53.
34. See Alfred Korzybski, *Science and Sanity; An Introduction to Non-Aristotelian Systems and General Semantics* (Lancaster: Science Press, Inc., 1941), Wendall Johnson, *People in Quandaries, the Sematics of Personal Adjustment* (New York: Harper and Brothers, 1946), and Kurt Lewin, *A Dynamic Theory of Personality* (New York: McGraw-Hill Inc., 1935).
35. Rousseau said, "Minds are formed by language." Rousseau, *op. cit.*, p. 73.
36. Rousseau, *op. cit.*, p. 73.
37. Rousseau, *op. cit.*, p. 62.
38. Rousseau, *op. cit.*, p. 84.
39. Rousseau, *op. cit.*, p. 44.
40. Rousseau, *op. cit.*, p. 72.
41. Rousseau, *op. cit.*, p. 125.
42. Rousseau, *op. cit.*, p. 53.
43. Rousseau, *op. cit.*, p. 155.
44. For Rousseau these included: (1) sensibility, (2) intelligence, and (3) will.
45. Rousseau, *op. cit.*, p. 140.
46. Rousseau, *op. cit.*, p. 165.
47. Rousseau, *op. cit.*, p. 143.
48. Rousseau was also practical enough to state: "Teach by doing whenever you can, and only fall back upon words when doing is out of the question." Rousseau, *op. cit.*, p. 144.
49. Rousseau, *op. cit.*, p. 174.
50. Rousseau, *op. cit.*, p. 174.
51. Rousseau, *op. cit.*, p. 197.

52. Rousseau, *op. cit.*, p. 217.
53. Rousseau, *op. cit.*, p. 90.
54. Rousseau, *op. cit.*, p. 134.
55. "Let students make their own maps, a very simple map at first, containing only two places; others may be added from time to time, as he is able to estimate their distance and position." Rousseau, *op. cit.*, p. 135.
56. Rousseau, *op. cit.*, p. 135.
57. Rousseau, *op. cit.*, p. 414ff.
58. Rousseau, *op. cit.*, p. 415ff.
59. "We cannot teach children the danger of telling lies to men without realizing, on the man's part, the danger of telling lies to children. A single untruth on the part of a teacher will destroy the results of his education." Rousseau, *op. cit.*, p. 177.
60. Rousseau, *op. cit.*, p. 177.
61. The Freudians, whom Rousseau anticipated in so many ways, would state that he had a complex regarding vagina supremacy.
62. A statement upon which he later contradicted himself.
63. He said, "In the present confusion between the sexes it is almost a miracle to belong to one's own sex." Rousseau, *op. cit.*, p. 356.
64. Rousseau, *op. cit.*, p. 326.
65. Rousseau, *op. cit.*, p. 327.
66. Rousseau, *op. cit.*, p. 328.
67. Rousseau, *op. cit.*, p. 329.
68. Rousseau, *op. cit.*, p. 331.
69. Rousseau, *op. cit.*, p. 349.
70. Rousseau, *op. cit.*, p. 340.
71. Rousseau, *op. cit.*, p. 45.
72. Rousseau did not follow the utopian tradition in regard to utilizing religious sanctions in character education. Rousseau did inject a section on religion and theology in the *Emile* under the guise of the creed of a Savoy priest. Rousseau's theology is inexact and confused. He attempted to follow Descartes by proceeding from doubt to faith. Rousseau said that the knowledge of God was common to all men and was strictly intuitive. Rousseau's faith was a form of religious optimism for he held in the *Emile* that the world was orderly and good per se. He stated that divine justice necessitated a life after death in order to adjust the inequalities of this life. Rousseau said that eternal happiness was a result of one's reflecting upon one's good deeds. Hell was a place of torment because one was forced to reflect upon his bad deeds. Rousseau believed in free will, and said that God would not help those that did wrong. Rousseau, *op. cit.*, p. 228ff.
73. Rousseau felt that it was harder to teach girls character education. Thus, he felt that their education in this area must begin before boys and must be more intense. Rousseau, *op. cit.*, p. 340.
74. Rousseau, *op. cit.*, p. 158.
75. Rousseau, *op. cit.*, p. 158.
76. Rousseau proposed in his limited form of education that the students he would have would all be from wealthy homes. He said that the children of poor families did not need his form of education; what they needed in the area of learning they would get from their parents. He felt that

the peasant parents, since they were closer to nature, would not need tutors since they were less likely to make mistakes as the wealthy class did.

77. Rousseau, *op. cit.*, p. 162.

78. For example, "Rousseau was a prophet of a new educational theory. *Emile,* in the history of literature, was one of the books which has had the most profound effect and its influence has been wide and lasting." Hudson, *op. cit.*, p. 201.

79. For a more detailed discussion of the use of the classics in modern educational practices see chapter IV.

80. Several of Rousseau's ideas have not been accepted because of their inherent impracticality; they include: a system of character education based upon selfishness, limiting education to a few, e.g., the wealthy and healthy, an isolated and controlled educational environment, a teacher system where the teacher spent at least twenty-five years with one student, a system of female education that was inferior to the male system.

81. There is a movement in several urban school systems to take whole classes for camping trips lasting up to several weeks. Some school systems, for example, Dearborn, Michigan, have purchased school camps. Teachers specially trained in camping education spend their time at the camp rather than in schools. However, this program has not as yet won general acceptance.

82. Rousseau did not discuss training in the professions, only in the manual trades.

83. Ernst Cassirer, *An Essay on Man, An Introduction to a Philosophy of Human Culture* (New York: Doubleday and Co., 1954), p. 181.

84. Babbitt, *op. cit.*, p. 268ff.

85. John W. Chapman, *Rousseau—Totalitarian or Liberal?* (New York: Columbia University Press, 1956).

86. Stuart Chase, *The Tyranny of Words* (New York: Harcourt, Brace, and Co., 1938), p. 237.

87. Immanuel Kant, *Critique of Pure Reason* (New York: Wiley Book Co., 1943), p. 1.

88. See Rousseau, *op. cit.*, p. 218, and Ernst Cassirer, *Rousseau, Kant and Goethe* (Princeton: Princeton University Press, 1947), p. 55.

89. Green, *op. cit.*, p. 264.

90. See Jean-Jacques Rousseau, *The Confessions* (New York: Pocket Books Inc., 1957).

91. Chapman, *op. cit.*, p. 142.

Chapter Eight

1. The traditional liberal movement operates in the main within the political framework of the state, whereas the radical movement operating within the social-cultural configuration demands an end of the political, economic, educational and even in some cases religious institutions within the state, and the inauguration of new institutions. Thus, while the anarchist wants no government, the radical wants government, but it must be in a new and different form.

2. More, *op. cit.*, p. 191.